Cake Mix
creations

Taste of Home BOOKS

READER'S DIGEST —
REIMAN MEDIA GROUP, INC.

Taste of Home · Reader's Digest

A TASTE OF HOME/READER'S DIGEST BOOK

©2014 Reiman Media Group, Inc., 5400 S. 60th St., Greendale WI 53129. All rights reserved.
Taste of Home and Reader's Digest are registered trademarks of The Reader's Digest Association, Inc.

EDITORIAL

Editor-in-Chief: Catherine Cassidy
Creative Director: Howard Greenberg
Editorial Operations Director: Kerri Balliet

Managing Editor, Print and Digital Books: Mark Hagen
Associate Creative Director: Edwin Robles Jr.

Editor: Janet Briggs
Art Director: Maggie Conners
Contributing Layout Designer: Siya Motamedi
Editorial Production Manager: Dena Ahlers
Copy Chief: Deb Warlaumont Mulvey
Copy Editor: Alysse Gear
Content Operations Manager: Colleen King
Content Operations Assistant: Shannon Stroud
Executive Assistant: Marie Brannon

Chief Food Editor: Karen Berner
Food Editors: James Schend; Peggy Woodward, RD
Associate Food Editor: Krista Lanphier
Associate Editor/Food Content: Annie Rundle
Recipe Editors: Mary King; Jenni Sharp, RD; Irene Yeh

Test Kitchen and Food Styling Manager: Sarah Thompson
Test Kitchen Cooks: Nicholas Iverson (lead), Matthew Hass, Lauren Knoelke
Prep Cooks: Megumi Garcia, Melissa Hansen, Nicole Spohrleder, Bethany Jacobson
Food Stylists: Kathryn Conrad (senior), Leah Rekau, Shannon Roum

Photography Director: Stephanie Marchese
Photographers: Dan Roberts, Jim Wieland
Photographer/Set Stylist: Grace Natoli Sheldon
Set Stylists: Stacey Genaw, Melissa Haberman, Dee Dee Jacq

Business Analyst: Kristy Martin
Billing Specialist: Mary Ann Koebernik

BUSINESS

General Manager, Taste of Home Cooking Schools: Erin Puariea

Vice President, Brand Marketing: Jennifer Smith
Vice President, Circulation and Continuity Marketing: Dave Fiegel

READER'S DIGEST NORTH AMERICA

Vice President, Business Development and Marketing: Alain Begun
President, Books and Home Entertainment: Harold Clarke
General Manager, Canada: Philippe Cloutier
Vice President, Operations: Mitch Cooper
Chief Operating Officer: Howard Halligan
Vice President, Chief Sales Officer: Mark Josephson
Vice President, General Manager, Milwaukee: Frank Quigley
Vice President, Digital Sales: Steve Sottile
Vice President, Chief Content Officer: Liz Vaccariello
Vice President, Global Financial Planning and Analysis: Devin White

THE READER'S DIGEST ASSOCIATION, INC.

President and Chief Executive Officer: Robert E. Guth

For other **Taste of Home books** and products, visit us at **tasteofhome.com.**

For more **Reader's Digest** products and information, visit **rd.com** (in the United States) or **rd.ca** (in Canada).

International Standard Book Number: 978-1-61765-278-3
Library of Congress Control Number: 2013917167

Cover Photographer: Grace Natoli Sheldon
Set Stylist: Stacey Genaw
Food Stylist: Leah Rekau

Pictured on front cover: Very Chocolate Torte with Raspberry Cream, page 17.
Pictured on back cover: Strawberry Angel Trifle, page 206; Banana Cream Brownie Dessert, page 242; Caramel Cashew Cake Pops, page 60.

PRINTED IN CHINA.
1 3 5 7 9 10 8 6 4 2

170

Butterscotch-Toffee Cheesecake Bars

{ Contents }

242

Mini Brownie Treats

Let Us Eat Cake...

and cookies, trifles, bars and other yummy sweets made from a cake mix!

It's easy to bake up scrumptious desserts—even when you're short on time! Weeknight surprises, bake sale contributions and classroom treats are a snap when you have a box of cake mix on hand!

Taste of Home Cake Mix Creations has **234 recipes** shared by family cooks who know how to cut kitchen time yet serve desserts that are big on flavor. These home bakers offer their secrets for whipping up layer cakes, tortes, cupcakes, cookies, bars and other fabulous treats, each of which stars a convenient cake mix.

Flip through this **colorful collection** and you'll find cakes to suit any occasion—from crowd pleasing snack cakes perfect for potlucks to impressive themed cakes sure to steal the show on holiday buffets. Need a cute birthday cake or a fun finale on July Fourth? See the **Party Cakes** chapter for clever ideas that come together in no time.

Nancy Horton has been baking her family's all-time favorite—Old-Fashioned Oat-Raisin Cookies—for more than 30 years! It's truly stood the test of time.

Cupcakes and cake pops are another reason to reach for a cake mix. Just stir in a few everyday ingredients for bakeshop-quality treats, such as **Caramel Cashew Cake Pops** and Lemon Meringue Cupcakes. With **Cake Mix Creations,** you'll save so much time that you can spend a little extra effort on decorating. Inside,

we'll show you how to turn cupcakes into silly monkeys, cute cats, fun clowns and so much more!

Cake mixes are also the base for **yummy cookies,** from macaroons and biscotti to sweet thumbprints and chip-filled stand-bys. And don't forget about bars! Cake mixes speed preparation on these snacks, too, featuring flavors such as **raspberry, lemon** and **peanut butter.**

You'll discover an entire chapter devoted to heavenly angel food cakes as well as a Bundt Cakes chapter filled with beautifully domed creations. In the Desserts & More section, you'll find effortless **coffee cakes, cinnamon rolls, crisps** and **trifles.** Best of all, a bonus chapter shows

you how to turn ordinary brownie mixes into extraordinary desserts such as cheesecakes and **even ice cream!**

Think you don't have time to surprise your family with an after-dinner delight? Grab a box of cake mix and look for the **quick–to–mix icon:** `FAST FIX` For these treats, you'll need no more than 15 minutes of hands-on prep work before setting things in the oven. What could be easier?

Turn your kitchen into the most popular bakeshop in town, and let your family and friends think you're a top baker. After all, there's no need to let them in on your little secret—a box of cake mix and **Cake Mix Creations!**

185

Old-Fashioned Oat-Raisin Cookies

Layer Cakes & Tortes

LEMON CREAM CAKE

Drizzling limoncello liqueur over the cake layers before frosting adds a tart punch.

—**AMY FREDERICK** ISLAND CITY, OR

PREP: 20 MIN.
BAKE: 25 MIN. + COOLING
MAKES: 12 SERVINGS

- 1 **package yellow cake mix (regular size)**
- 1¼ **cups water**
- 3 **eggs**
- ⅓ **cup canola oil**
- 1 **teaspoon lemon extract**
- 1 **carton (8 ounces) mascarpone cheese**
- 1 **cup heavy whipping cream**
- ½ **cup lemon curd**
- ¼ **cup limoncello, optional**
  Fresh raspberries and lemon peel strips

1. In a large bowl, combine cake mix, water, eggs, oil and extract; beat on low speed for 30 seconds. Beat on medium for 2 minutes. Pour into two greased and floured 9-in. round baking pans.

2. Bake at 350° for 22-26 minutes or until a toothpick inserted near the center comes out clean. Cool for 10 minutes before removing from the pans to wire racks to cool completely.

3. In a small bowl, beat the cheese, cream and lemon curd until smooth. Place one cake layer on a serving plate. Drizzle with half the limoncello if desired; spread with half the cheese mixture. Repeat layers. Garnish with raspberries and lemon peel. Store in the refrigerator.

CHOCOLATE-ALMOND SACHER TORTE

Each bite of this luscious cake features the delightful flavors of chocolate, almonds and apricots.

—TASTE OF HOME TEST KITCHEN

PREP: 30 MIN. • **BAKE:** 25 MIN. + CHILLING • **MAKES:** 12-16 SERVINGS

½ cup chopped dried apricots
½ cup amaretto
1 package devil's food cake mix (regular size)
¾ cup water
⅓ cup canola oil
3 eggs

APRICOT FILLING
⅔ cup apricot preserves
1 tablespoon amaretto

FROSTING
½ cup butter, softened
4½ cups confectioners' sugar
¾ cup baking cocoa
⅓ cup boiling water
1 tablespoon amaretto
1 cup sliced almonds, toasted

1. In a small bowl, combine the apricots and amaretto; let stand for 15 minutes. In a large bowl, combine the cake mix, water, oil, eggs and apricot mixture. Beat on low speed for 30 seconds; beat on medium for 2 minutes. Pour into two greased and floured 9-in. round baking pans.

2. Bake at 350° for 25-30 minutes or until a toothpick inserted near the center comes out clean. Cool for 10 minutes before removing from the pans to wire racks to cool completely.

3. For filling, in a small saucepan, heat the apricot preserves and amaretto on low until preserves are melted, stirring occasionally; set aside.

4. For frosting, in a large bowl, cream the butter, confectioners' sugar and cocoa until smooth.

Add water and amaretto. Beat on low speed until combined. Beat on medium for 1 minute or until frosting achieves spreading consistency.

5. Cut each cake horizontally into two layers. Place a bottom layer on a serving plate; spread with half of the filling. Top with another cake layer; spread with ⅔ cup frosting. Top with third layer and remaining filling. Top with remaining cake layer.

6. Frost top and sides of cake with remaining frosting. Gently press almonds into the sides. Refrigerate for several hours before slicing.

PECAN PEAR TORTE

This delicious pear-flavored cake is topped with butterscotch whipped cream and will be a showstopper when you present it to family or guests.

—**JEANNE HOLT** MENDOTA HEIGHTS, MN

PREP: 25 MIN. • **BAKE:** 20 MIN. + COOLING • **MAKES:** 10 SERVINGS

- 1 **can (15 ounces) pear halves**
- 1 **package butter recipe golden cake mix (regular size)**
- ½ **cup butter, softened**
- 3 **eggs**
- 1 **teaspoon vanilla extract**
- ½ **cup chopped pecans, toasted**

TOPPING

- 1 **carton (8 ounces) frozen whipped topping, thawed**
- ⅔ **cup butterscotch ice cream topping, divided**
- 2 **cups chopped peeled ripe pears**
- 1 **tablespoon lemon juice**
- ⅓ **cup pecan halves, toasted**

1. Drain pears, reserving liquid. Puree the pears in a blender; add enough of the reserved liquid to measure 1 cup.

2. In a large bowl, combine the cake mix, butter, eggs, vanilla, chopped pecans and pear puree; beat on low speed for 30 seconds. Beat on medium for 2 minutes. Pour into two greased and floured 9-in. round baking pans.

3. Bake at 375° for 20-25 minutes or until a toothpick inserted near the center comes out clean. Cool for 10 minutes before removing from pans to wire racks to cool completely.

4. In a small bowl, fold whipped topping into ⅓ cup butterscotch topping. Place one cake layer on a serving plate. Spread with half of the filling. Toss pears with lemon juice; sprinkle half of the pears over the filling. Drizzle with 2 tablespoons of the butterscotch topping. Repeat layers.

5. Arrange pecan halves on top of cake. Drizzle with the remaining butterscotch topping. Store in the refrigerator.

NOTE *Butterscotch topping should be at room temperature.*

COME-HOME-TO-MAMA CHOCOLATE CAKE

Using a mix, it will take you less than a half hour to whip up this cure-all cake. Sour cream and chocolate pudding make it rich and moist, and chocolate, chocolate and more chocolate make it decadent comfort food at its finest.
—TASTE OF HOME TEST KITCHEN

PREP: 25 MIN. • **BAKE:** 40 MIN. + COOLING • **MAKES:** 12 SERVINGS

- 1 **package devil's food cake mix (regular size)**
- 1 **cup (8 ounces) sour cream**
- 1 **package (3.9 ounces) instant chocolate fudge pudding mix**
- 4 **eggs**
- ⅓ **cup canola oil**
- ¼ **cup water**
- ¼ **cup buttermilk**
- 2 **tablespoons chocolate syrup**
- 2 **teaspoons vanilla extract**

FROSTING
- 1 **pound semisweet chocolate, chopped**
- 6 **tablespoons Dutch-process cocoa powder**
- 6 **tablespoons boiling water**
- 1½ **cups butter, softened**
- ½ **cup confectioners' sugar**

1. In a large bowl, combine the first nine ingredients; beat on low speed for 30 seconds. Beat on medium for 2 minutes. Pour the batter into two greased and floured 8-in. baking pans.

2. Bake at 350° for 38-43 minutes or until a toothpick inserted near the center comes out clean. Cool for 10 minutes before removing from the pans to wire racks to cool completely.

3. For frosting, in a microwave, melt chocolate; stir until smooth.

Let chocolate cool to room temperature, about 20-30 minutes. Meanwhile, dissolve cocoa in boiling water; cool.

4. In a large bowl, beat butter and confectioners' sugar until fluffy. Add melted chocolate; beat on low speed until combined, scraping sides of the bowl as needed. Beat in cocoa mixture.

5. Place one cake layer on a serving plate; spread with 1½ cups frosting. Top with the remaining cake layer. Spread the remaining frosting over top and sides of cake.

CHOCOLATE MINT CREAM CAKE

I had a lot of fun dreaming up my fun dessert. It's easy but very impressive when serving. The peppermint gives the cookies-and-cream flavor a cool holiday spin.

—PATTY THOMPSON JEFFERSON, IA

PREP: 30 MIN. • **BAKE:** 20 MIN. + COOLING • **MAKES:** 14 SERVINGS

- 1 **package white cake mix (regular size)**
- 1 **cup water**
- ½ **cup canola oil**
- 3 **eggs**
- ½ **teaspoon peppermint extract**
- 1 **cup crushed mint creme Oreo cookies**

TOPPING

- 2 **packages (3.9 ounces each) instant chocolate pudding mix**
- ⅓ **cup confectioners' sugar**
- 1½ **cups cold 2% milk**
- ½ **to 1 teaspoon peppermint extract**
- 1 **carton (12 ounces) frozen whipped topping, thawed**
- ½ **cup crushed mint creme Oreo cookies**
- 15 **mint Andes candies**

1. In a large bowl, combine the cake mix, water, oil, eggs and extract; beat on low speed for 30 seconds. Beat on medium speed for 2 minutes. Fold in crushed cookies. Pour into three greased and floured 9-in. round baking pans.

2. Bake at 350° for 18-24 minutes or until a toothpick inserted near the center comes out clean. Cool for 10 minutes before removing from the pans to wire racks to cool completely.

3. For topping, combine the dry pudding mixes, confectioners' sugar, milk and extract until thickened. Fold in whipped topping and crushed cookies.

4. Place one cake layer on a serving plate; spread with the topping. Repeat layers twice. Frost the sides of cake with the remaining topping.

5. Chop eight candies; sprinkle over center of cake. Cut the remaining candies in half; garnish each serving with a half candy. Store in the refrigerator.

FAST FIX ▶ PEACH CAKE

My mom's springtime layer cake is peachy and creamy.
My brother, whose birthday is in April, requests Mom's specialty every year.

—TAMRA DUNCAN LINCOLN, AR

PREP: 15 MIN. • **BAKE:** 30 MIN. + COOLING • **MAKES:** 10-12 SERVINGS

- 1 **can (15¼ ounces) sliced peaches, undrained**
- 1 **package yellow cake mix (regular size)**
- ⅓ **cup canola oil**
- 3 **eggs**
- 1 **carton (8 ounces) frozen whipped topping, thawed**
- ¾ **cup (6 ounces) peach yogurt Additional drained diced peaches, if desired**

1. Drain peaches, reserving juice. Add enough water to juice to measure 1¼ cups. Cut peaches into 1-in. pieces; set aside.

2. In a large bowl, beat the cake mix, peach juice mixture, oil and eggs on low speed for 30 seconds. Beat on medium for 2 minutes. Pour into two greased and floured 9-in. round baking pans.

3. Bake at 350° for 28-33 minutes or until a toothpick inserted near the center comes out clean. Cool in pans for 10 minutes before removing to wire racks to cool completely.

4. In a bowl, combine the whipped topping and yogurt; fold in the reserved peaches. Spread topping between layers and over top of cake. Garnish with additional diced peaches if desired. Store in refrigerator.

PUMPKIN SPICE LAYER CAKE

Perfect for fall holidays, the warm, aromatic spices of cinnamon, ginger and nutmeg along with the pumpkin will make you think of the brilliant hues of autumn leaves.

—LINDA MURRAY ALLENSTOWN, NH

PREP: 25 MIN. • **BAKE:** 25 MIN. + COOLING • **MAKES:** 10-12 SERVINGS

- 1 **package yellow cake mix (regular size)**
- 3 **eggs**
- 1 **cup water**
- 1 **cup canned pumpkin**
- 1¾ **teaspoons ground cinnamon, divided**
- ¼ **teaspoon ground ginger**
- ¼ **teaspoon ground nutmeg**
- 2½ **cups vanilla frosting**
- 1¼ **cups chopped walnuts**

1. In a large bowl, combine the cake mix, eggs, water, pumpkin, 1 teaspoon cinnamon, ginger and nutmeg; beat on low speed for 30 seconds. Beat on medium for 2 minutes. Pour into two well-greased and floured 9-in. round baking pans.

2. Bake at 375° for 25-30 minutes or until a toothpick inserted near the center comes out clean. Cool for 10 minutes before removing from the pans to wire racks to cool completely.

3. Combine frosting and remaining cinnamon; spread between layers and over top and sides of cake. Press walnuts lightly into frosting on sides of cake.

STRAWBERRY CAKE

To hint at the flavor of this fresh-tasting strawberry cake with its pretty pink tint before cutting, garnish the top with whole strawberries.

—PAM ANDERSON BILLINGS, MT

PREP: 25 MIN. • **BAKE:** 25 MIN. + COOLING • **MAKES:** 12-16 SERVINGS

- 1 **package white cake mix (regular size)**
- 1 **package (3 ounces) strawberry gelatin**
- 1 **cup water**
- ½ **cup canola oil**
- 4 **egg whites**
- ½ **cup mashed unsweetened strawberries**
  Whipped cream or frosting for your choice

1. In a large bowl, combine the dry cake mix, gelatin powder, water and oil. Beat on low speed for 1 minute or until moistened; beat on medium for 4 minutes.

2. In a small bowl with clean beaters, beat egg whites on high speed until stiff peaks form. Fold egg whites and mash strawberries into cake batter. Pour into three greased and floured 8-in. round baking pans.

3. Bake at 350° for 25-30 minutes or until a toothpick comes out clean. Cool for 10 minutes before removing from pans to wire racks to cool completely.

4. Frost with whipped cream or frosting. If frosted with whipped cream, store in the refrigerator.

RASPBERRY ORANGE TORTE

Guests are sure to be dazzled by this sensational dessert that's ideal for special occasions. A rich orange cream filling is spread between the cake layers for a luscious look and taste.

—TASTE OF HOME TEST KITCHEN

PREP: 25 MIN. • **BAKE:** 30 MIN. + COOLING • **MAKES:** 10-12 SERVINGS

- 1 **package white cake mix (regular size)**
- 1 **package (10 ounces) frozen sweetened raspberries, thawed**
- 2 **cups heavy whipping cream**
- 1 **carton (8 ounces) mascarpone cheese**
- ¾ **cup sugar**
- 2 **tablespoons orange juice**
- ½ **teaspoon grated orange peel**
- 2 **cups fresh raspberries**

1. Prepare and bake the cake according to package directions, using two greased and floured 9-in. round baking pans. Cool for 10 minutes before removing from the pans to a wire rack to cool completely.

2. Press sweetened raspberries through a sieve; discard seeds. Set raspberry puree aside. In a small bowl, beat cream until stiff peaks form. In a large bowl, beat the mascarpone cheese, sugar, orange juice and orange peel. Fold in the whipped cream.

3. Cut each cake into two horizontal layers. Place bottom layer on a serving plate. Brush with about ¼ cup raspberry puree. Spread with about 1 cup cream mixture; top with ½ cup fresh raspberries. Repeat the layers three times. Store in the refrigerator.

MARVELOUS CANNOLI CAKE

A luscious, chocolate-studded cannoli filling separates the tender vanilla layers of this wonderful cake. It's best served well chilled.

—ANTOINETTE OWENS RIDGEFIELD, CT

PREP: 30 MIN. + CHILLING • **BAKE:** 25 MIN. + COOLING • **MAKES:** 12 SERVINGS

1 package French vanilla cake mix (regular size)

FILLING

- 1 carton (16 ounces) ricotta cheese
- ½ cup confectioners' sugar
- 2 teaspoons ground cinnamon
- 1 teaspoon almond extract
- 1 teaspoon rum extract
- 1 teaspoon vanilla extract
- 2 ounces semisweet chocolate, finely chopped

FROSTING

- 2 cartons (8 ounces each) mascarpone cheese
- ¾ cup confectioners' sugar, sifted
- ¼ cup whole milk
- 2 teaspoons almond extract
- 1 teaspoon vanilla extract
- 1 cup sliced almonds
- 2 tablespoons miniature semisweet chocolate chips

1. Prepare and bake cake mix according to package directions, using two greased and floured 9-in. round baking pans. Cool for 10 minutes before removing from pans to wire racks to cool completely.

2. In a large bowl, combine the ricotta cheese, confectioners' sugar, cinnamon and extracts; stir in chocolate. In another bowl, beat the mascarpone cheese, confectioners' sugar, milk and extracts on medium speed until creamy (do not overmix).

3. Place one cake layer on a serving plate; spread with 1 cup filling. Top with second cake layer. Spread remaining filling over top of cake to within 1 inch of edges. Frost sides and top edge of cake with 2 cups frosting.

4. Press almonds into sides of cake. Sprinkle chocolate chips over top. Store in the refrigerator.

RED, WHITE & BLUEBERRY POKE CAKE

A sweet treat in the summer, this patriotic poke cake with
dazzling red and blue stripes is a fun one to make with the kids.

—ELISABETH SCHULZ BLOSSVALE, NY

PREP: 40 MIN. + COOLING • **BAKE:** 25 MIN. + CHILLING • **MAKES:** 12 SERVINGS

- 1 **package white cake mix (regular size)**
- 1¼ **cups water**
- 2 **eggs**
- ¼ **cup canola oil**

STRAWBERRY GELATIN
- 1 **cup fresh strawberries**
- ¼ **cup water**
- ⅔ **cup sugar**
- 2¼ **teaspoons strawberry gelatin**

BLUEBERRY GELATIN
- ¾ **cup fresh blueberries**
- ½ **cup water**
- 4½ **teaspoons sugar**
- 4½ **teaspoons berry blue gelatin**

FROSTING AND FILLING
- 2½ **cups heavy whipping cream**
- ⅓ **cup confectioners' sugar**

1. Line bottoms of two 9-in. round baking pans with parchment or waxed paper; coat paper with cooking spray. In a large bowl, beat the cake mix, water, eggs and oil; beat on low speed for 30 seconds. Beat on medium for 2 minutes. Pour into prepared pans.

2. Bake at 350° for 25-30 minutes or until a toothpick inserted near the center comes out clean. Cool completely in pans on wire racks.

3. For the strawberry gelatin, in a small saucepan, combine the strawberries, water and sugar; bring to a boil. Reduce heat; simmer, uncovered, for 2-3 minutes or until berries are soft. Strain into a small bowl, pressing berries lightly; discard pulp. Add the gelatin to syrup, stirring to dissolve completely. Cool to room temperature. Repeat steps to make blueberry gelatin.

4. Using a wooden skewer, pierce tops of cakes to within 1 inch of edge; twist skewer gently to make slightly larger holes. Gradually pour cooled strawberry mixture over one cake, being careful to fill each hole. Repeat with blueberry mixture and remaining cake. Refrigerate, covered, overnight.

5. In a large bowl, beat cream until it begins to thicken. Add confectioners' sugar; beat until soft peaks form.

6. Run a knife around edges of pans to loosen cakes. Remove strawberry cake from pan; remove paper. Place on a serving plate. Spread with 1 cup whipped cream.

7. Remove blueberry cake from pan; remove paper. Place cake over whipped cream layer. Frost top and sides with remaining cream. Chill for at least 1 hour before serving. Refrigerate the leftovers.

VERY CHOCOLATE TORTE WITH RASPBERRY CREAM

Here's a way to take a simple cake mix and make it look spectacular! The filling and frosting are really quite easy to make so there's no reason to shy away from this dessert.

—TASTE OF HOME TEST KITCHEN

PREP: 30 MIN. • **BAKE:** 20 MIN. + COOLING • **MAKES:** 16 SERVINGS

2 packages chocolate cake mix

FROSTING

- **2 cups (12 ounces) semisweet chocolate chips**
- **½ cup butter, cubed**
- **1 cup (8 ounces) sour cream**
- **4½ cups confectioners' sugar**

RASPBERRY FILLING

- **½ cup heavy whipping cream**
- **¼ cup red raspberry preserves**
- **1½ teaspoons sugar**
- **1 teaspoon raspberry liqueur**

DECORATIONS

- **2 ounces white baking chocolate, chopped**
  Chocolate curls and fresh raspberries

1. Prepare and bake cake mixes according to package directions, using four 9-in. round baking pans.

2. For frosting, in a small heavy saucepan, melt chocolate chips and butter over low heat; stir until smooth. Transfer to a large bowl; cool 5 minutes. Stir in sour cream. Gradually beat in confectioners' sugar until smooth.

3. For filling, in a small bowl, beat cream until it begins to thicken. Add preserves, sugar and liqueur; beat until stiff peaks form.

4. Save one cake layer for another use. Using a long serrated knife, cut each remaining cake layer horizontally in half. Place one layer on a serving plate; spread with about ⅓ cup filling. Top with another cake layer; spread with

½ cup frosting. Repeat layers. Top with another cake layer, remaining filling and remaining cake layer. Frost top and sides of cake with remaining frosting.

5. Melt white chocolate in a microwave; stir until smooth. Place mixture in a resealable plastic bag; cut a small hole in a

corner of bag. Pipe over top of cake as desired. Refrigerate until serving. Just before serving, top with the chocolate curls and raspberries. Store leftovers in the refrigerator.

NOTE *The drizzle for this recipe was tested with Ghirardelli white chocolate.*

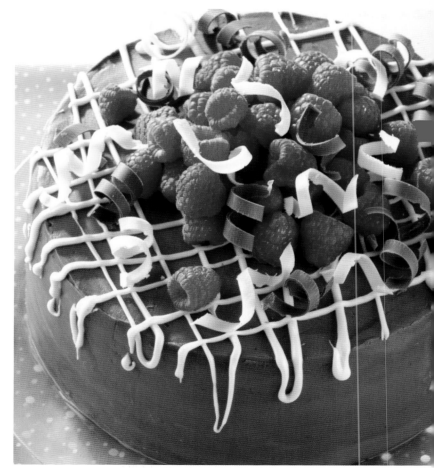

CHOCOLATE-STRAWBERRY CELEBRATION CAKE

Although I have some great from-scratch recipes, this one uses a boxed mix with plenty of doctoring. It has become a popular groom's cake that gets more attention than the wedding cake.

—NORA FITZGERALD SEVIERVILLE, TN

PREP: 30 MIN. • **BAKE:** 30 MIN. + COOLING • **MAKES:** 12 SERVINGS

- 1 **package chocolate cake mix (regular size)**
- 1 **package (3.9 ounces) instant chocolate pudding mix**
- 4 **eggs**
- 1 **cup (8 ounces) sour cream**
- ¾ **cup water**
- ¼ **cup canola oil**
- 4 **ounces semisweet chocolate, melted**

FROSTING
- 2 **cups butter, softened**
- 4 **cups confectioners' sugar**
- ¾ **cup baking cocoa**
- ½ **cup 2% milk**

GANACHE
- 4 **ounces semisweet chocolate, chopped**
- ½ **cup heavy whipping cream**

GARNISHES
- 2 **ounces semisweet chocolate, melted**
- 1 **pound fresh strawberries, hulled**

1. Combine the first seven ingredients; beat on low speed for 30 seconds. Beat on medium for 2 minutes. Transfer to two greased and floured 9-in. round baking pans.

2. Bake at 350° for 28-32 minutes or until a toothpick inserted near the center comes out clean. Cool for 10 minutes before removing from pans to wire racks to cool completely.

3. In a large bowl, cream the butter, confectioner's sugar and cocoa until light and fluffy. Beat in the milk until smooth. Spread the frosting between layers and over top and sides of cake.

4. For ganache, place chocolate in a small bowl. Heat cream just to a boil; pour over chocolate and whisk until smooth. Drizzle over top of cake, allowing ganache to drape down the sides.

5. Pipe or spoon the melted chocolate onto waxed paper in decorative designs; let stand until set. Arrange the strawberries on top of cake. Top with chocolate garnishes.

DARK CHOCOLATE-CARROT CAKE

Carrot cake has a dark side—and it's divine! Cream cheese adds richness, while toasted nuts and cinnamon boost the flavor.

—DARLENE BRENDEN SALEM, OR

PREP: 20 MIN.
BAKE: 25 MIN. + COOLING
MAKES: 16 servings

- 1 **package dark chocolate cake mix (regular size)**
- 4 **ounces cream cheese, softened**
- 1 **package (3.9 ounces) instant chocolate pudding mix**
- 1 **cup 2% milk**
- 3 **eggs**
- 1 **teaspoon ground cinnamon**
- 3 **cups shredded carrots**
- 1 **cup chopped walnuts, toasted, divided**
- 2 **cans (16 ounces each) cream cheese frosting**

1. In a large bowl, combine cake mix, cream cheese, pudding mix, milk, eggs and cinnamon; beat on low speed for 30 seconds. Beat on medium for 2 minutes. Stir in the carrots and ½ cup walnuts. Pour into three greased and floured 8-in. round baking pans.

2. Bake at 350° for 25-30 minutes or until a toothpick inserted near the center comes out clean. Cool for 10 minutes before removing from pans to wire racks to cool completely.

3. Spread frosting between layers and over top and sides of cake. Sprinkle top with remaining walnuts. Store in the refrigerator.

CRANBERRY ORANGE CAKE

Here's a bright and lovely addition for the end of a meal. Mayonnaise is the secret ingredient that gives this cake its marvelous texture.

—TASTE OF HOME TEST KITCHEN

PREP: 30 MIN. + CHILLING • **BAKE:** 25 MIN. + COOLING • **MAKES:** 14 SERVINGS

1 **package yellow cake mix (regular size)**
1¼ **cups mayonnaise**
4 **eggs**
¼ **cup orange juice**

FILLING
⅓ **cup whole-berry cranberry sauce**
¼ **cup cranberry juice**
4 **teaspoons cranberry gelatin powder**
½ **cup whipped topping**
½ **teaspoon grated orange peel**

FROSTING
1 **package (8 ounces) cream cheese, softened**
1 **jar (7 ounces) marshmallow creme**
⅛ **teaspoon almond extract**
1½ **cups whipped topping**

1. In a large bowl, beat the cake mix, mayonnaise, eggs and orange juice until well blended. Transfer to two greased and floured 9-in. round baking pans.

2. Bake at 350° for 25-30 minutes or until a toothpick inserted near the center comes out clean. Cool for 10 minutes; remove from pans to wire racks to cool completely.

3. For filling, in a large saucepan, bring cranberry sauce and juice to a boil; cook and stir until blended. Stir in the gelatin powder until dissolved. Cool slightly; transfer to a small bowl. Refrigerate for 30 minutes or until mixture begins to thicken. Fold in the whipped topping and orange peel.

4. For the frosting, in a large bowl, beat the cream cheese until fluffy. Add marshmallow creme and extract; beat until smooth. Beat in the whipped topping.

5. Place one cake layer on a serving plate; spread with half of the filling. Top with remaining cake layer. Spread 2 cups frosting over top and sides of cake. Spread remaining filling over top of cake to within 1 inch of edges. Pipe the remaining frosting around edge of cake. Store in the refrigerator.

CINNAMON & SUGAR CAKE

This winning combination makes everything nice with sugar and spice.
Your guests will never know it started with a mix unless you let the secret slip out.
—**MAIAH MILLER** CARLSBAD, CA

PREP: 25 MIN. • **BAKE:** 20 MIN. + COOLING • **MAKES:** 12 SERVINGS

- 1 **package white cake mix (regular size)**
- 1 **cup 2% milk**
- ½ **cup sour cream**
- 6 **tablespoons butter, melted**
- 3 **eggs**
- 2½ **teaspoons ground cinnamon**
- 1½ **teaspoons vanilla extract**

FROSTING
- 1 **cup butter, softened**
- 5 **cups confectioners' sugar**
- 2 **tablespoons 2% milk**
- 1 **teaspoon ground cinnamon**
- 1 **teaspoon vanilla extract**
- 1 **tablespoon cinnamon-sugar**

1. In a large bowl, combine the first seven ingredients; beat on low speed for 30 seconds. Beat on medium for 2 minutes. Transfer batter to two greased and floured 9-in. round baking pans.

2. Bake at 350° for 20-25 minutes or until a toothpick inserted near the middle comes out clean. Cool for 10 minutes before removing from the pans to wire racks to cool completely.

3. In a large bowl, beat butter until fluffy. Add confectioners' sugar, milk, cinnamon and extract; beat until smooth. Spread the frosting between layers and over top and sides of cake. Sprinkle with cinnamon-sugar. Store in the refrigerator.

RASPBERRY COCONUT CAKE

This seemed like a festive dessert to fix for the holidays,
so I decided to first try it out on my co-workers. They loved it!

—JOANIE WARD BROWNSBURG, IN

PREP: 20 MIN. • **BAKE:** 25 MIN. + COOLING • **MAKES:** 12 SERVINGS

1 **package white cake mix (regular size)**
3 **cups flaked coconut, divided**
6 **ounces white baking chocolate, chopped**
¼ **cup heavy whipping cream**
¾ **cup seedless raspberry jam**
1 **cup butter, softened**
1 **cup confectioners' sugar**

1. Prepare cake batter according to package directions; fold in ⅔ cup coconut. Pour into two greased and floured 9-in. round baking pans.

2. Bake at 350° for 25-30 minutes or until a toothpick inserted near the center comes out clean. Cool for 10 minutes before removing from the pans to wire racks to cool completely.

3. In a microwave, melt white chocolate with cream at 70% power for 1 minute; stir. Microwave at 10- to 20-second intervals, stirring until smooth. Cool to room temperature.

4. In a bowl, combine jam and 1 cup coconut. Spread over one cake layer; top with second layer.

5. In a small bowl, beat butter until fluffy. Add confectioners' sugar; beat until smooth. Gradually beat in white chocolate mixture. Spread over top and sides of cake. Toast remaining coconut; press over top and sides of cake.

NOTE *This recipe was tested in a 1,100-watt microwave.*

WHITE CHOCOLATE COCONUT CAKE

The white snowball look makes this cute cake the perfect choice
for a Christmas celebration or other wintertime party.
—**GRETA KIRBY** CARTHAGE, TN

PREP: 25 MIN. + CHILLING • **BAKE:** 25 MIN. + COOLING • **MAKES:** 12 SERVINGS

- 1 **package white cake mix (regular size)**
- 1 **cup water**
- 1 **can (15 ounces) cream of coconut, divided**
- 3 **egg whites**
- 1 **can (5 ounces) evaporated milk**
- ⅔ **cup white baking chips**
- 2 **ounces cream cheese, softened**
- 1 **cup heavy whipping cream, divided**
- 3½ **cups flaked coconut, divided**
- 2 **teaspoons vanilla extract, divided**
- ¼ **cup sugar**

1. In a large bowl, combine the cake mix, water, ¾ cup cream of coconut and egg whites; beat on low speed for 30 seconds. Beat on medium for 2 minutes. Pour into three greased and floured 9-in. round baking pans.

2. Bake at 350° for 22-26 minutes or until a toothpick inserted near the center comes out clean. Cool for 10 minutes before removing from the pans to wire racks to cool completely.

3. For filling, in a small saucepan, combine evaporated milk, chips, cream cheese, 3 tablespoons heavy cream and the remaining cream of coconut; cook and stir over low heat until the chips are melted.

4. Remove from the heat; stir in 1½ cups coconut and 1 teaspoon vanilla. Transfer to a large bowl; cover and refrigerate until the mixture reaches spreading consistency, stirring occasionally.

5. For frosting, in a large bowl, beat remaining cream until it begins to thicken. Add sugar and remaining vanilla; beat until stiff peaks form.

6. Place bottom cake layer on a serving plate; spread with half of the filling. Repeat layers. Top with remaining cake layer. Frost top and sides of cake; sprinkle with remaining coconut. Store in the refrigerator.

SUSAN'S FAVORITE MOCHA CAKE

My family insists on my mocha cake for our holiday dinner.
They call it the best cake in the world. The layors of flavor are flawless.

—SUSAN BAZAN SEQUIM, WA

PREP: 30 MIN. • **BAKE:** 25 MIN. + CHILLING • **MAKES:** 16 SERVINGS

- 1 **package chocolate cake mix (regular size)**
- 1¾ **cups sour cream**
- 2 **eggs**
- ½ **cup coffee liqueur**
- ¼ **cup canola oil**
- 2 **cups (12 ounces) semisweet chocolate chips, divided**
- 1 **package (10 to 12 ounces) white baking chips**
- ⅓ **cup butter, cubed**
- 1 **tablespoon instant coffee granules**
- 1 **teaspoon rum extract**
- 1 **envelope unflavored gelatin**
- 1½ **cups heavy whipping cream, divided**

WHIPPED CREAM

- 2 **cups heavy whipping cream**
- ½ **cup sugar**
- 1 **teaspoon vanilla extract**

1. In a large bowl, combine the cake mix, sour cream, eggs, liqueur and oil; beat on low speed for 30 seconds. Beat on medium for 2 minutes. Stir in 1 cup chocolate chips. Pour into three greased and floured 9-in. round baking pans.

2. Bake at 350° for 24-28 minutes or until a toothpick inserted near the center comes out clean. Cool for 10 minutes before removing from the pans to wire racks to cool completely.

3. In a microwave, melt white baking chips, butter and the remaining chocolate chips; stir until smooth. Stir in the coffee granules and extract. Cool to room temperature.

4. In a small saucepan, sprinkle gelatin over ¼ cup cream; let stand for 1 minute. Heat over low heat, stirring until the gelatin is completely dissolved. Stir into chocolate mixture. In a large bowl, beat the remaining 1¼ cups cream until soft peaks form. Add to the cooled chocolate mixture; beat until stiff peaks form.

5. For whipped cream, in a small bowl, beat cream until it begins to thicken. Add sugar and vanilla; beat until stiff peaks form.

6. Place bottom cake layer on a serving plate; top with half of the chocolate mixture. Repeat layers. Top with remaining cake layer. Frost top and sides of cake with whipped cream. Refrigerate for at least 2 hours before serving.

LEMON RASPBERRY-FILLED CAKE

This attractive sweet tastes as good as it looks. It's special enough for company...
but your guests might not believe you that it's light!

—HEIDI SCOTT APPLETON, WI

PREP: 15 MIN. • **BAKE:** 20 MIN. + COOLING • **MAKES:** 12 SERVINGS

- 1 **package lemon cake mix (regular size)**
- 2 **eggs**
- 1 **egg white**
- 1¼ **cups water**
- ¼ **cup unsweetened applesauce**

FROSTING

- 2 **cups confectioners' sugar**
- 2 **tablespoons butter, softened**
- 1 **teaspoon vanilla extract**
- ⅛ **teaspoon salt**
- 2 **to 3 tablespoons fat-free milk**
- ½ **cup 100% raspberry spreadable fruit**

1. In a large bowl, combine the cake mix, eggs, egg white, water and applesauce; beat on low speed for 30 seconds. Beat on medium for 2 minutes. Pour into two 9-in. round baking pans coated with cooking spray.

2. Bake at 350° for 20-30 minutes or until a toothpick inserted near the center comes out clean. Cool pans on wire racks for 10 minutes; remove from the pans to cool completely.

3. For frosting, in a large bowl, beat first four frosting ingredients until smooth. Beat in enough milk to reach desired consistency.

4. Place one cake layer on a serving plate. Spread with the spreadable fruit. Top with second layer; frost top of cake.

CHOCOLATE-PRALINE LAYER CAKE

For the chocolate lover in all of us, this is the peak of cocoa heaven. Packed with pecans, the luscious layers are topped off with heart-shaped chocolate candies. Every day is Valentine's Day with this cake!

—KATHY ENGLER BROOKFIELD, WI

PREP: 30 MIN. • **BAKE:** 30 MIN.+ COOLING • **MAKES:** 12 SERVINGS

- 1 **cup packed brown sugar**
- ½ **cup butter, cubed**
- ¼ **cup heavy whipping cream**
- ¾ **cup coarsely chopped pecans**

CAKE

- 1 **package chocolate cake mix (regular size)**
- 4 **eggs**
- 1 **cup fat-free milk**
- ½ **cup butter, softened**
- ½ **cup sweetened condensed milk**
- 1 **package (3.4 ounces) cook-and-serve chocolate pudding mix**

TOPPING

- 1¾ **cups heavy whipping cream**
- ¼ **cup confectioners' sugar**
- ¼ **teaspoon vanilla extract**
    Heart-shaped chocolate candies

1. In a small heavy saucepan, combine brown sugar, butter and cream. Cook and stir over medium heat until the sugar is dissolved. Pour into two greased 9-in. round baking pans and sprinkle with the pecans.

2. In a large bowl, beat the cake mix, eggs, milk, butter, sweetened condensed milk and pudding mix; beat on low speed for 30 seconds. Beat on medium for 2 minutes. Transfer to prepared pans.

3. Bake at 350° for 30-35 minutes or until a toothpick inserted near the center comes out clean. Cool for 10 minutes before removing

from the pans to wire racks to cool completely.

4. In a large bowl, beat cream until it begins to thicken. Add confectioners' sugar and vanilla; beat until stiff peaks form.

5. Place one cake layer on a serving plate, praline side up. Spread with half of the whipped cream. Top with remaining cake layer; spread remaining whipped cream over top. Garnish with candies. Store in the refrigerator.

RASPBERRY BUTTER TORTE

Raspberry pie filling and homemade chocolate frosting jazz up a cake mix to create a picture-perfect torte. With a hint of rum flavor, it's rich and creamy for special occasions but so fun and simple to do, you could prepare it on weeknights, too.

—TASTE OF HOME TEST KITCHEN

PREP: 30 MIN. • **BAKE:** 30 MIN. + COOLING • **MAKES:** 12-14 SERVINGS

- 1 **package butter recipe golden cake mix (regular size)**
- ¼ **cup chopped almonds, toasted**
- 2 **cups heavy whipping cream**
- 1 **cup confectioners' sugar**
- ¼ **cup baking cocoa**
- 1½ **teaspoons rum extract**
- 2 **cups raspberry cake and pastry filling**
  Chocolate curls
  Sliced almonds, toasted, optional

1. Prepare cake batter according to package directions; fold in the chopped almonds. Pour into two greased and floured 9-in. round baking pans. Bake as directed. Cool for 10 minutes before removing from pans to wire racks to cool completely.

2. For frosting, in a small bowl, beat cream until it begins to thicken. Add the confectioners' sugar, cocoa and extract; beat until stiff peaks form.

3. Cut each cake into two horizontal layers. Place one layer on a serving plate; spread with ½ cup raspberry filling and ½ cup frosting. Repeat with remaining cake layers.

4. Place remaining frosting in a pastry bag with a star tip #195. Decorate top and sides of cake as desired. Garnish with chocolate curls. Sprinkle with the sliced almonds if desired. Store in the refrigerator.

NOTE *To duplicate the look of the cake in the picture above, pipe about ½ cup of the frosting around the cake between each layer and 1½ cups of the frosting on top.*

FAST FIX PINEAPPLE LAYER CAKE

I often prepare this tender, golden cake at Easter, but it's wonderful at any time of year. Pineapple frosting provides a fast, fresh finishing touch.
—**LINDA SAKAL** BILOXI, MS

PREP: 15 MIN. • **BAKE:** 25 MIN. + COOLING • **MAKES:** 12 SERVINGS

1 **package yellow cake mix (regular size)**
1 **can (11 ounces) mandarin oranges, drained**
1 **can (20 ounces) unsweetened crushed pineapple, drained**
1 **package (3.4 ounces) instant vanilla pudding mix**
1 **package (12 ounces) frozen whipped topping, thawed**

1. Prepare cake batter according to package directions. Beat in oranges until blended. Pour into two greased and floured 9-in. round baking pans.

2. Bake at 350° for 25-30 minutes or until a toothpick inserted near the center comes out clean. Cool for 10 minutes before removing from the pans to wire racks to cool completely.

3. Combine pineapple and dry pudding mix; fold in whipped topping. Spread between layers and over top and sides of cake. Store in the refrigerator.

ALMOND CHOCOLATE TORTE

I've been making this recipe since the '70s, and it's often requested by family and friends. It's popular not only for the wonderful eye appeal and taste, but for the short time it takes to assemble.
—**ELAINE GAIRY** CHESTER, MD

PREP: 30 MIN. • **BAKE:** 35 MIN. + CHILLING • **MAKES:** 12 SERVINGS

1 **package chocolate cake mix (regular size)**
12 **ounces German sweet chocolate, chopped**
¾ **cup butter, cubed**
½ **cup chopped almonds, toasted**
1 **carton (8 ounces) frozen whipped topping, thawed Chocolate curls**

1. Prepare and bake the cake according to package directions, using two greased and floured 9-in. round baking pans. Cool for 10 minutes before removing from the pans to wire racks to cool completely.

2. Meanwhile, in a small saucepan, melt chocolate and butter; stir until smooth. Stir in almonds (mixture will be thin); set aside.

3. Split each cake into two horizontal layers. Place bottom layer on a serving plate; spread with half of the chocolate mixture. Top with second cake layer; spread with half of the whipped topping. Repeat layers. Sprinkle with chocolate curls. Chill at least 1 hour before serving. Refrigerate leftovers.

FAST FIX ▶ SWEET POTATO LAYER CAKE

Crushed pineapple adds a subtle fruity flavor to this tasty layered cake.
The silky cream cheese frosting is ia delicious complement.

—JOYCE WALTER NICHOLASVILLE, KY

PREP: 15 MIN. • **BAKE:** 20 MIN. + COOLING • **MAKES:** 12 SERVINGS

1 **package yellow cake mix (regular size)**
1 **can (15 ounces) sweet potatoes, drained and mashed**
1 **cup water**
½ **cup all-purpose flour**
2 **eggs**
1 **can (8 ounces) unsweetened crushed pineapple, well drained**
2 **tablespoons canola oil**
1 **teaspoon ground cinnamon**
1 **teaspoon vanilla extract**
½ **teaspoon ground nutmeg**
FROSTING
2 **packages (8 ounces each) cream cheese, softened**
½ **cup butter, softened**
2 **teaspoons vanilla extract**
7½ **cups confectioners' sugar**

1. In a large bowl, mix first 10 ingredients. Beat on low speed for 30 seconds. Beat on medium 2 minutes. Divide batter among three greased and floured 9-in. round baking pans.

2. Bake at 350° for 20-25 minutes or until a toothpick inserted near the center comes out clean. Cool for 10 minutes before removing from pans to wire racks to cool completely.

3. For frosting, in a large bowl, beat the cream cheese, butter and vanilla until fluffy. Gradually beat in the confectioners' sugar until smooth. Spread between layers and over top and sides of cake. Store in the refrigerator.

CARROT-SPICE CAKE WITH CARAMEL FROSTING

My special treat is loaded with extras to give it that from-scratch flavor.
It's so delectable that everyone asks for the recipe!

—NORA FITZGERALD SEVIERVILLE, TN

PREP: 45 MIN. • **BAKE:** 25 MIN. + COOLING • **MAKES:** 12 SERVINGS

- 1 **package spice cake mix (regular size)**
- 1 **package (3.4 ounces) instant vanilla pudding mix**
- 4 **eggs**
- ¾ **cup water**
- ½ **cup sour cream**
- ¼ **cup canola oil**
- 1 **cup shredded carrots**
- 1 **can (8 ounces) unsweetened crushed pineapple, drained**
- ½ **cup flaked coconut**
- ½ **cup chopped pecans**
- ¼ **cup raisins**

FROSTING
- 1 **cup butter, softened**
- 1 **package (8 ounces) cream cheese, softened**
- 6 **cups confectioners' sugar**
- ½ **cup caramel ice cream topping**
- 1 **to 2 tablespoons 2% milk**

1. In a large bowl, combine the cake mix, pudding mix, eggs, water, sour cream and oil; beat on low speed for 30 seconds. Beat on medium for 2 minutes. Fold in the carrots, pineapple, coconut, pecans and raisins just until blended. Pour into two greased and floured 9-in. round baking pans.

2. Bake at 350° for 25-30 minutes or until a toothpick inserted near the center comes out clean. Cool for 10 minutes before removing from the pans to wire racks to cool completely.

3. For frosting, in a large bowl, beat butter and cream cheese until fluffy. Add confectioners' sugar, ice cream topping and enough milk to reach desired consistency. Spread the frosting between layers and over the top and sides of the cake. Store in the refrigerator.

EASY BLUE-RIBBON PEANUT BUTTER TORTE

No one will guess that this tall, tiered cake isn't completely homemade. Chunky peanut butter is stirred into both the cake batter and the decadent chocolate ganache, giving each layer a rich, from-scratch taste.

—TASTE OF HOME TEST KITCHEN

PREP: 25 MIN. + CHILLING • **BAKE:** 20 MIN. + COOLING • **MAKES:** 14 SERVINGS

- 1 **package yellow cake mix (regular size)**
- 1¼ **cups water**
- 1 **cup chunky peanut butter, divided**
- 3 **eggs**
- ⅓ **cup canola oil**
- 1 **teaspoon vanilla extract**
- 1 **package (10 ounces) 60% cacao bittersweet chocolate baking chips**
- 2¼ **cups heavy whipping cream**
- ½ **cup packed brown sugar**
- 2 **cans (16 ounces each) cream cheese frosting**
- 2 **Butterfinger candy bars (2.1 ounces each), coarsely chopped**
- ⅓ **cup chopped honey-roasted peanuts**

1. Grease and flour three 9-in. round baking pans; set aside. Combine the cake mix, water, ½ cup peanut butter, eggs, oil and vanilla in a large bowl; beat on low speed for 30 seconds. Beat on medium for 2 minutes. Pour the batter into prepared pans (pans will have a shallow fill).

2. Bake at 350° for 17-20 minutes or until a toothpick inserted in the center comes out clean. Cool for 10 minutes before removing from pans to wire racks.

3. Place chocolate chips in a large bowl. Bring cream and brown sugar to a boil in a small heavy saucepan over medium heat, stirring occasionally. Reduce heat; simmer for 1-2 minutes or until sugar is dissolved.

4. Pour cream mixture over chocolate; whisk until smooth. Stir in remaining peanut butter until blended. Chill until mixture reaches a spreading consistency. Spread between layers.

5. Frost top and sides of cake. Garnish with the chopped candy bars and peanuts. Store in the refrigerator.

NOTE *Reduced-fat peanut butter is not recommended for this recipe.*

BLUEBERRY CITRUS CAKE

My husband and I grow blueberries for market, and this cake is my favorite way to use them.
Our fresh berries are enhanced by the light, citrusy frosting. I bring this beauty to all potlucks.
—SHIRLEY COOPER SALEMBURG, NC

PREP: 40 MIN. • **BAKE:** 20 MIN. + COOLING • **MAKES:** 12 SERVINGS

1 package yellow cake mix
(regular size)
3 eggs
1 cup orange juice
⅓ cup canola oil
1½ cups fresh blueberries
1 tablespoon grated lemon peel
1 tablespoon grated orange
peel

CITRUS FROSTING

1 package (3 ounces) cream
cheese, softened
¼ cup butter, softened
3 cups confectioners' sugar
2 tablespoons orange juice

2 teaspoons grated orange peel
1 teaspoon grated lemon peel
2 cups whipped topping

1. In a large bowl, combine the cake mix, eggs, orange juice and oil; beat on low speed for 30 seconds. Beat on medium for 2 minutes. Fold in blueberries and peels. Pour into two greased and floured 9-in. round baking pans.

2. Bake at 350° for 20-25 minutes or until a toothpick inserted near the center comes out clean. Cool for 10 minutes before removing from the pans to wire racks to cool completely.

3. For frosting, in a small bowl, beat cream cheese and butter until fluffy. Add confectioners' sugar, orange juice and peels; beat until blended. Fold in the whipped topping.

4. Spread frosting between layers and over the top and sides of cake. Store in the refrigerator.

RED VELVET CREPE CAKES

It's well worth the time to make this beautiful and delicious cake. Each thin layer is separated by a rich, creamy filling. Your holiday dessert spread will totally dazzle—even without sparklers!

—CRYSTAL HEATON ALTON, UT

PREP: 1¼ HOURS • **COOK:** 25 MIN. • **MAKES:** 2 CREPE CAKES (8 SERVINGS EACH)

- 1 **package red velvet cake mix (regular size)**
- 2¾ **cups whole milk**
- 1 **cup all-purpose flour**
- 3 **eggs**
- 3 **egg yolks**
- ¼ **cup butter, melted**
- 3 **teaspoons vanilla extract**

FROSTING

- 5 **packages (3 ounces each) cream cheese, softened**
- 1¼ **cups butter, softened**
- ½ **teaspoon salt**
- 12 **cups confectioners' sugar**
- 5 **teaspoons vanilla extract**
  Fresh blueberries

1. In a large bowl, combine the cake mix, milk, flour, eggs, egg yolks, butter and vanilla; beat on low speed for 30 seconds. Beat on medium for 2 minutes.

2. Heat a lightly greased 8-in. nonstick skillet over medium heat; pour ¼ cup batter into center of skillet. Lift and tilt pan to coat bottom evenly. Cook until top appears dry; turn and cook 15-20 seconds longer. Remove to a wire rack. Repeat with the remaining batter, greasing skillet as needed. When cool, stack the crepes with waxed paper or paper towels in between.

3. For frosting, in a large bowl, beat cream cheese, butter and salt until fluffy. Add confectioners' sugar and vanilla; beat until smooth.

4. To assemble two crepe cakes, place one crepe on each of two cake plates. Spread each with one rounded tablespoon frosting to within ½ inch of edges. Repeat layers until all crepes are used. Spread remaining frosting over tops and sides of crepe cakes. Garnish with blueberries. Store in the refrigerator.

TRUFFLE-TOPPED CAKE

This eye-catching dessert will be the talk of the party; especially if guests find out how easy it is to make! Store-bought truffles and chopped hazelnuts add holiday pizazz to a simple yellow cake mix.

—TASTE OF HOME TEST KITCHEN

PREP: 30 MIN. • **BAKE:** 25 MIN. + COOLING • **MAKES:** 12 SERVINGS

1 **package yellow cake mix (regular size)**
1 **cup butter, softened**
1 **jar (12¼ ounces) caramel ice cream topping**
3 **tablespoons milk**
1½ **teaspoons vanilla extract**
6 **cups confectioners' sugar**
¾ **cup chopped hazelnuts**
  Assorted truffles

1. Prepare and bake the cake according to package directions, using two greased 9-in. square baking pans. Cool for 10 minutes before removing from pans to wire racks to cool completely.

2. For frosting, in a large bowl, beat butter until light. Beat in caramel topping, milk and vanilla until smooth. Gradually beat in confectioners' sugar until smooth.

3. Place one cake layer on a serving plate; spread with 1 cup frosting. Top with remaining cake layer. Frost top and sides of cake with remaining frosting. Press hazelnuts into sides of cake. Top cake with truffles.

NOTE *This recipe was tested with Ferrero Rocher truffles.*

MOCHA CREAM TORTE

My guests would never imagine that I didn't spend all day in the kitchen making this impressive chocolate cake. Mocha flavor and cream cheese frosting make it special.

—MARY LONSE CHATFIELD, MN

PREP: 30 MIN. • **BAKE:** 20 MIN. + COOLING • **MAKES:** 12-16 SERVINGS

- 1½ cups graham cracker crumbs
- ¾ cup packed brown sugar
- ½ cup butter, melted
- ½ cup chopped walnuts
- 1 tablespoon mocha-flavored coffee drink mix
- 1 package dark chocolate cake mix (regular size)

FROSTING

- 1 package (8 ounces) cream cheese, softened
- 2 tablespoons butter, softened
- 2 tablespoons sour cream
- 3 tablespoons mocha-flavored coffee drink mix
- 4 cups confectioners' sugar

1. Grease and flour three 9-in. round baking pans. Line bottoms with waxed paper; grease and flour the paper. In a small bowl, mix cracker crumbs, brown sugar, butter, walnuts and drink mix; press into prepared pans.

2. Prepare cake batter according to package directions; pour over prepared crusts. Bake according to package directions. Cool for 10 minutes; remove from pans to wire racks to cool completely. Remove waxed paper.

3. For frosting, in a large bowl, beat the cream cheese, butter, sour cream and drink mix until fluffy. Add confectioners' sugar; beat until smooth.

4. Place one cake layer, crunchy side up, on a serving plate. Spread with ¾ cup frosting. Repeat with remaining layers and frosting. Store in the refrigerator.

NOTE *This recipe was tested with Pillsbury dark chocolate cake mix.*

LEMON POPPY SEED CAKE

This lovely layered cake may not be made from scratch, but lemon curd filling and creamy frosting give it a gourmet flair. It's a refreshing change from chocolate holiday desserts.

—SUZANNE EARL SPRING, TX

PREP: 40 MIN. • **BAKE:** 25 MIN. + COOLING • **MAKE:** 12 SERVINGS

- 3 **eggs, separated**
- 1 **package lemon cake mix (regular size)**
- 1 **cup 2% milk**
- ⅓ **cup buttermilk**
- ⅓ **cup canola oil**
- ¼ **cup unsweetened applesauce**
- ¼ **cup lemon juice**
- 1 **tablespoon grated lemon peel**
- 4 **teaspoons poppy seeds**
- 2 **cups heavy whipping cream**
- ¼ **cup sugar**
- 2 **teaspoons vanilla extract**
- 1 **jar (10 ounces) lemon curd**

1. Place egg whites in a large bowl; let stand at room temperature for 30 minutes.

2. In another large bowl, combine the cake mix, milk, buttermilk, oil, applesauce, lemon juice, egg yolks, lemon peel and poppy seeds; beat on low speed for 30 seconds. Beat on medium for 2 minutes. In another bowl, beat egg whites until stiff peaks form; fold into batter. Transfer to two greased and floured 9-in. round baking pans.

3. Bake at 350° for 22-28 minutes or until a toothpick inserted near the center comes out clean. Cool for 10 minutes before removing from the pans to wire racks to cool completely.

4. In a large bowl, beat cream until it begins to thicken. Add sugar and vanilla; beat until stiff peaks form.

5. Cut each cake horizontally into two layers. Place bottom layer on a serving plate; top with ⅓ cup lemon curd. Repeat layers twice. Top with remaining cake layer. Spread remaining lemon curd over top of cake within 1 inch of edges. Frost sides and top edge of cake with 3 cups whipped cream mixture. Pipe remaining mixture around edges.

TO MAKE AHEAD *The cake layers can be made the day before serving. Store in resealable plastic bags at room temperature.*

BANANA FLIP CAKE

Here's a recipe that will bring back memories of your childhood.
This cake tastes just like the banana flips we used to eat when we were kids.

—BERTA HAGEN INTERNATIONAL FALLS, MN

PREP: 30 MIN. • **BAKE:** 30 MIN. + COOLING • **MAKES:** 16 SERVINGS

- 1 **package yellow cake mix (regular size)**
- 1 **package (3.4 ounces) instant banana or vanilla pudding mix**
- 1½ **cups 2% milk**
- 4 **eggs**

FROSTING

- ⅓ **cup all-purpose flour**
- 1 **cup 2% milk**
- ½ **cup butter, softened**
- ½ **cup shortening**
- 1 **cup sugar**
- 1½ **teaspoons vanilla extract**
- 2 **tablespoons confectioners' sugar**

1. Line two greased 15x10x1-in. baking pans with waxed paper and grease the paper. Set aside. In a large bowl, combine the cake mix, pudding mix, milk and eggs. Beat on low speed for 30 seconds; beat on medium for 2 minutes.

2. Spread batter into prepared pans. Bake at 350° for 12-15 minutes or until a toothpick inserted near the centers come out clean. Cool for 5 minutes before inverting onto wire racks to cool completely. Gently peel off waxed paper.

3. Meanwhile, in a small saucepan, whisk the flour and milk until smooth. Bring to a boil; cook and stir for 2 minutes or until thickened. Remove from the heat; cover and cool to room temperature.

4. In the bowl of a heavy-duty stand mixer, cream the butter, shortening and sugar until light and fluffy. Beat in vanilla. Add milk mixture; beat on high for 10-15 minutes or until fluffy.

5. Place one cake on a large cutting board; spread top with frosting. Top with remaining cake; sprinkle with confectioners' sugar. Cut into slices. Store in the refrigerator.

{2}

Cupcakes

43

Cookie Dough Cupcakes with Ganache Frosting

60

Caramel Cashew Cake Pops

73

Fruit-Filled Cupcakes

BOSTON CREAM PIE CUPCAKES

My favorite hockey team, the Boston Bruins, inspired me to make these creative cupcakes when they won the Stanley Cup in 2011. I like to decorate them with a "B" but you can add a love note on top with a little white icing.
—**ALISA CHRISTENSEN** RANCHO SANTA MARGARITA, CA

PREP: 30 MIN. + CHILLING • **BAKE:** 20 MIN. + COOLING • **MAKES:** 20 CUPCAKES

- 1 **package yellow cake mix (regular size)**
- 1 **package (3.4 ounces) cook-and-serve chocolate pudding mix**

GLAZE
- ⅔ **cup semisweet chocolate chips**
- 2½ **tablespoons butter**
- 1¼ **cups confectioners' sugar**
- 3 **tablespoons hot water**
  White decorating icing, optional

1. Prepare and bake the cake mix according to the package directions for cupcakes, using 20 paper-lined muffin cups. Cool completely.

2. Meanwhile, in a small bowl, prepare pudding mix according to the package directions. Press plastic wrap onto surface of pudding; refrigerate until cold.

3. Cut a small hole in the tip of a pastry bag or in a corner of a food-safe plastic bag; insert a small pastry tip. Transfer pudding to bag. Using a wooden or metal skewer, poke a hole through bottom of cupcake liners. Push tip through hole and pipe filling into cupcakes.

4. In a microwave, melt the chocolate chips and butter; stir until smooth. Whisk in the confectioners' sugar and water. Dip tops of cupcakes into glaze. If desired, pipe designs on cupcakes with white icing..

HOT CHOCOLATE CAKE BALLS

Serve these chocolaty delights, and everyone will know yours isn't an ordinary holiday party.
The little cakes are festive, fun and yummy.
—TASTE OF HOME TEST KITCHEN

PREP: 1¼ HOURS + CHILLING • **BAKE:** 30 MIN. + COOLING • **MAKES:** 5 DOZEN

1 package chocolate cake mix (regular size)
1¼ cups strong brewed coffee
⅓ cup canola oil
3 eggs

FILLING
¾ cup butter, softened
1 cup confectioners' sugar
¼ teaspoon vanilla extract
1 jar (7 ounces) marshmallow creme

FROSTING
¼ cup butter, softened
2 cups confectioners' sugar
¼ cup baking cocoa
¼ cup 2% milk
½ teaspoon vanilla extract

COATING
2 pounds white candy coating, chopped
1 tablespoon shortening
Baking cocoa

1. In a large bowl, combine cake mix, coffee, oil and eggs; beat on low speed for 30 seconds. Beat on medium for 2 minutes. Pour the batter into a greased and floured 13-in. x 9-in. baking pan.

2. Bake at 350° for 30-35 minutes or until a toothpick inserted near the center comes out clean. Cool cake completely.

3. For filling, in a small bowl, beat the butter until fluffy; beat in the confectioners' sugar and vanilla until smooth. Add marshmallow creme; beat until light and fluffy. Refrigerate for at least 2 hours or until easy to handle. Shape into ½-in. balls; arrange on waxed paper-lined baking sheets.

4. For frosting, in a large bowl, beat the butter, confectioners' sugar and cocoa until combined. Beat in milk and vanilla until smooth. Crumble cake into bowl; mix well.

5. Shape 1 tablespoon cake mixture around a marshmallow ball. Return to baking sheets. Repeat with the remaining cake mixture and marshmallow balls. Refrigerate for 30 minutes.

6. In a microwave, melt candy coating and shortening; stir until smooth. Dip cake balls in coating; allow excess to drip off. Return to baking sheets; let stand until set. Dust tops with cocoa. Store cake balls in an airtight container in the refrigerator.

TIE-DYED CUPCAKES

Take a trip back to the sixties with these sweet psychedelic cupcakes. Each is a simple white cake, but tinting the batter all the colors of the rainbow makes them funky and fun!
—**GWYNDOLYN WILKERSON** KYLE, TX

PREP: 30 MIN. • **BAKE:** 25 MIN. + COOLING • **MAKES:** 1½ DOZEN

1 **package white cake mix (regular size)**
1½ cups **(12 ounces) lemon-lime soda**
 Neon food coloring
1 **can (16 ounces) vanilla frosting**
 Colored sprinkles

1. In a large bowl, combine cake mix and soda. Beat on low speed for 30 seconds. Beat on medium for 1 minute. Divide batter among five bowls. Add a few drops of food coloring to each bowl; stir just until combined.

2. Drop a spoonful of one color of batter into each of 18 paper-lined muffin cups. Layer with the remaining colored batter until muffin cups are two-thirds full.

3. Bake at 350° for 18-20 minutes or until a toothpick inserted near the center comes out clean. Cool for 10 minutes before removing from the pans to wire racks to cool completely.

4. Frost the tops and decorate with sprinkles.

NOTE *In this recipe, lemon-lime soda is used in place of the water, egg whites and oil typically used when preparing white cake mix. One-and-a-half cups (12 ounces) diet lemon-lime soda can be used instead of regular soda for a lower-sugar option.*

COOKIE DOUGH CUPCAKES WITH GANACHE FROSTING

I created this recipe using one of my favorite guilty pleasures, cookie dough, and a traditional yellow cupcake. The chocolaty frosting adds extra flavor to this unbeatable dessert. What's not to love?

—**MORGAN PHILLIPS** CHARLOTTESVILLE, VA

PREP: 25 MIN. + CHILLING • **BAKE:** 15 MIN. • **MAKES:** 2 DOZEN

- 1 **package yellow cake mix (regular size)**
- 1 **cup milk**
- 3 **eggs**
- ½ **cup butter, melted**
- 1 **teaspoon vanilla extract**
- 1 **tube (16½ ounces) refrigerated chocolate chip cookie dough**

FROSTING

- 2 **cups (12 ounces) semisweet chocolate chips**
- 1 **cup heavy whipping cream**
- ½ **cup miniature semisweet chocolate chips**

1. In a large bowl, combine the cake mix, milk, eggs, butter and vanilla; beat on low speed for 30 seconds. Beat on medium for 2 minutes.

2. Fill paper-lined muffin cups one-third full. Roll tablespoonfuls of cookie dough into balls. Drop into center of each cupcake. Top with remaining batter.

3. Bake at 350° for 15-20 minutes or until a toothpick comes out clean. Cool for 10 minutes before removing from pans to wire racks to cool completely.

4. For frosting, in a small saucepan, melt chocolate chips with cream over low heat; stir until blended. Remove from the heat. Transfer to a small bowl; cover and refrigerate for 45-60 minutes or until mixture reaches spreading consistency, stirring every 15 minutes.

5. Cut a small hole in the corner of pastry or plastic bag; insert #20 star pastry tip. Fill bag with the chocolate mixture; pipe onto cupcakes. Sprinkle with the miniature chocolate chips.

HEAVENLY CHOCOLATE-FUDGE CAKE BALLS

My special treat is similar to the popular cake pops—but without the stick! They're guaranteed to calm any chocolate craving and jazz up holiday goodie trays all at the same time. Best of all, no one will guess how easy they are to make.

—LYNN DAVIS MORENO VALLEY, CA

PREP: 1¾ HOURS + STANDING • **BAKE:** 30 MIN. + COOLING • **MAKES:** ABOUT 8 DOZEN

- 1 **package devil's food cake mix (regular size)**
- 2 **tablespoons hot water**
- 1 **teaspoon instant coffee granules**
- 1 **cup chocolate fudge frosting**
- ⅓ **cup baking cocoa**
- ¼ **cup chocolate syrup**
- 1⅓ **cups miniature semisweet chocolate chips**
- 2 **pounds white candy coating, chopped**
  Optional toppings: milk chocolate English toffee bits, toasted flaked coconut and crushed candy canes

1. Prepare and bake the cake according to package directions. Cool completely. Crumble cake into a large bowl.

2. In a small bowl, combine hot water and coffee granules; stir until dissolved. Add the frosting, cocoa and chocolate syrup; stir until combined. Add to the cake; beat on low speed until blended. Stir in chocolate chips. Shape into 1-in. balls.

3. In a microwave, melt candy coating; stir until smooth. Dip balls in coating mixture; allow excess to drip off. Place on waxed paper; sprinkle with toppings of your choice. Let stand until set. Store in airtight containers.

CREEPY CUPCAKES

These are so fun to whip up and eat. It looks like the worms are crawling out of dirt, and the spiders look like they're resting on the cupcakes. Even adults can't resist getting in on the fun!

—JOYCE MOYNIHAN LAKEVILLE, MN

PREP: 30 MIN. • **BAKE:** 20 MIN. + COOLING • **MAKES:** 2 DOZEN

1 **package chocolate cake mix (regular size)**
WORMY CUPCAKES
1 **can (16 ounces) chocolate frosting**
20 **Oreo cookies, crushed**
24 **gummy worms, halved**
SPIDER CUPCAKES
1 **can (16 ounces) vanilla frosting**
Orange paste food coloring
24 **Oreo Cookies**

Red or black shoestring licorice
48 **milk chocolate M&Ms**

1. Prepare and bake cake batter according to package directions for cupcakes. Cool completely.

2. *For wormy cupcakes,* set aside 1 tablespoon frosting. Frost the cupcakes with the remaining frosting; dip each into crushed cookies. Place a dab of reserved frosting on the cut end of each

worm half; place two on each cupcake.

3. *For spider cupcakes,* in a small bowl, tint frosting orange; set aside 1 tablespoon. Frost cupcakes with remaining frosting. Place one cookie on each cupcake.

4. For legs, cut licorice into 2-in. pieces; press eight pieces into each cupcake. Attach two M&M's to each cookie for eyes, using reserved frosting.

RASPBERRY TRUFFLE CAKE POPS

Rich chocolate with a hint of raspberry liqueur...it doesn't get any better than this!

—TASTE OF HOME TEST KITCHEN

PREP: 1½ HOURS + FREEZING • **MAKES:** 4 DOZEN

- **1 package white cake mix (regular size)**
- **½ cup canned vanilla frosting**
- **⅓ cup seedless raspberry jam, melted**
- **2 to 3 tablespoons raspberry liqueur**
  Red food coloring, optional
- **48 lollipop sticks**
- **2½ pounds dark chocolate candy coating, chopped**
  Pink candy coating, chopped
  Pink sprinkles and decorative sugar, optional

1. Prepare and bake cake mix according to package directions, using a greased 13-in. x 9-in. baking pan. Cool completely on a wire rack.

2. Crumble cake into a large bowl. Add the frosting, jam, liqueur and food coloring if desired; mix well. Shape into 1-in. balls. Place on baking sheets; insert sticks. Freeze for at least 2 hours or refrigerate for at least 3 hours or until cake balls are firm.

3. In a microwave, melt dark candy coating. Dip each cake pop in coating; allow excess to drip off. Insert cake pops into a plastic foam block to stand. Melt pink candy coating; drizzle over cake pops. Decorate some cake pops with sprinkles and sugar if desired. Let stand until set.

GERMAN CHOCOLATE CUPCAKES

These cupcakes disappear in a flash when I take them to the school where I teach.
The coconut-pecan topping dresses them up nicely, so no one misses the icing.
—LETTICE CHARMASSON SAN DIEGO, CA

PREP: 20 MIN. • **BAKE:** 15 MIN. + COOLING • **MAKES:** ABOUT 2 DOZEN

- **1 package German chocolate cake mix (regular size)**
- **1 cup water**
- **3 eggs**
- **½ cup canola oil**
- **3 tablespoons chopped pecans**
- **3 tablespoons flaked coconut**
- **3 tablespoons brown sugar**

1. In a large bowl, combine the cake mix, water, eggs and oil. Beat on low speed for 30 seconds. Beat on medium for 2 minutes.

2. Fill paper-lined muffin cups three-fourths full. Combine the pecans, coconut and brown sugar; sprinkle over batter.

3. Bake at 400° for 15-20 minutes or until a toothpick inserted near the center comes out clean. Cool for 10 minutes before removing from the pans to wire racks to cool completely.

BERRY SURPRISE CUPCAKES

These cupcakes have a surprise inside them—Fruit Roll-Ups.
They give the cupcakes a sweet, fruity flavor.
The treats are sure to be a hit at any get-together.
—SUSAN LUCAS BRAMPTON, ON

PREP: 20 MIN. • **BAKE:** 15 MIN. + COOLING • **MAKES:** 2 DOZEN

1 **package white cake mix (regular size)**
1⅓ **cups water**
3 **egg whites**
2 **tablespoons canola oil**
3 **strawberry Fruit Roll-Ups, unrolled**
1 **can (16 ounces) vanilla frosting**
6 **pouches strawberry Fruit Snacks**

1. In a large bowl, combine cake mix, water, egg whites and oil. Beat on low speed for 30 seconds. Beat on medium for 2 minutes.

2. Fill paper-lined muffin cups half full. Cut each fruit roll into eight pieces; place one piece over batter in each cup. Fill two-thirds full with remaining batter.

3. Bake at 350° for 15-20 minutes or until a toothpick inserted near the center comes out clean. Cool for 10 minutes before removing from the pans to wire racks to cool completely. Frost with the vanilla frosting; decorate with the Fruit Snacks.

NOTE *This recipe was tested with Betty Crocker Fruit Roll-Ups and Nabisco Fruit Snacks.*

CREAMY CENTER CUPCAKES

My mother made these cupcakes from scratch when I was growing up. I simplified them with a cake mix.
Sometimes Mom would replace the smooth filling with homemade whipped cream. They're great with either filling.
—CAROLINE ANDERSON WAUPACA, WI

PREP: 45 MIN. + COOLING • **MAKES:** 2 DOZEN

1 **package devil's food cake mix (regular size)**
¾ **cup shortening**
⅔ **cup confectioners' sugar**
1 **cup marshmallow creme**
1 **teaspoon vanilla extract**
2 **cans (16 ounces each) chocolate frosting**

1. Prepare and bake the cake mix according to package directions for cupcakes, using paper-lined muffin cups. Cool for 10 minutes before removing from pans to wire racks to cool completely.

2. Meanwhile in a large bowl, the cream shortening and sugar until light and fluffy. Beat in the marshmallow creme and vanilla.

3. Cut a small hole in the corner of a pastry or plastic bag; insert a very small round tip. Fill with cream filling. Push tip through bottom of paper liner to fill each cupcake. Frost with chocolate frosting.

LEMON MERINGUE CUPCAKES

Classic lemon meringue pie inspired these gorgeous little cupcakes. The tangy treats hide a surprise lemon pie filling and are topped with fluffy toasted meringue. Make them for your next special gathering.

—**ANDREA QUIROZ** CHICAGO, IL

PREP: 30 MIN. • **BAKE:** 25 MIN. + COOLING • **MAKES:** 2 DOZEN

1 **package lemon cake mix (regular size)**
1⅓ **cups water**
⅓ **cup canola oil**
3 **eggs**
1 **tablespoon grated lemon peel**
1 **cup lemon creme pie filling**
MERINGUE
3 **egg whites**
½ **teaspoon cream of tartar**
½ **cup sugar**

1. In a large bowl, combine the cake mix, water, oil, eggs and lemon peel; beat on low speed for 30 seconds. Beat on medium for 2 minutes. Fill paper-lined muffin cups two-thirds full.

2. Bake at 350° for 18-22 minutes or until a toothpick inserted near the center comes out clean.

3. Cut a small hole in the corner of a pastry or plastic bag; insert a very small round tip. Fill with pie filling. Push the tip into the top of each cupcake to fill.

4. In a large bowl, beat egg whites and cream of tartar on medium speed until soft peaks form. Gradually beat in the sugar, 1 tablespoon at a time, on high until stiff glossy peaks form and sugar is dissolved. Pipe over tops of cupcakes.

5. Bake at 400° for 5-8 minutes or until meringue is golden brown. Cool for 10 minutes before removing from pans to wire racks to cool completely. Store in an airtight container in the refrigerator.

CHOCOLATE ANGEL CUPCAKES WITH COCONUT CREAM FROSTING

Sweeten any meal with these fun, frosted chocolate cupcakes that take just minutes to make. The finger-licking flavor packs far fewer calories and fat than traditional desserts!

—MANDY RIVERS LEXINGTON, SC

PREP: 15 MIN. • **BAKE:** 15 MIN. + COOLING • **MAKES:** 2 DOZEN

1 package (16 ounces) angel food cake mix
¾ cup baking cocoa
1 cup (8 ounces) reduced-fat sour cream
1 cup confectioners' sugar
⅛ teaspoon coconut extract
2½ cups reduced-fat whipped topping
¾ cup flaked coconut, toasted

1. Prepare cake mix according to package directions for cupcakes, adding cocoa when mixing.

2. Fill foil- or paper-lined muffin cups two-thirds full. Bake at 375° for 11-15 minutes or until the cake springs back when lightly touched and cracks in top feel dry. Cool for 10 minutes before removing from the pans to wire racks to cool completely.

3. For frosting, in a large bowl, combine the sour cream, confectioners' sugar and extract until smooth. Fold in whipped topping. Frost cupcakes. Sprinkle with the coconut. Store in the refrigerator.

TRES LECHES CUPCAKES

Infused with a sweet silky mixture using a trio of milks, these little cakes are three times as good. Because they soak overnight, they're an ideal make-ahead dessert for an upcoming fiesta.

—TASTE OF HOME TEST KITCHEN

PREP: 45 MIN. + CHILLING • **BAKE:** 20 MIN. + COOLING • **MAKES:** 2 DOZEN

- 1 **package yellow cake mix (regular size)**
- 1¼ **cups water**
- 4 **eggs**
- 1 **can (14 ounces) sweetened condensed milk**
- 1 **cup coconut milk**
- 1 **can (5 ounces) evaporated milk**
  Dash salt
  Whipped cream and assorted fresh fruit

1. In a large bowl, combine the cake mix, water and eggs; beat on low speed for 30 seconds. Beat on medium for 2 minutes. Fill paper-lined muffin cups two-thirds full.

2. Bake at 350° for 18-22 minutes or until a toothpick inserted near the center comes out clean. Cool for 10 minutes before removing from the pans to wire racks to cool completely.

3. Combine the sweetened condensed milk, coconut milk, evaporated milk and salt. Using the end of a wooden spoon handle, poke a hole into the center of each cupcake. Transfer milk mixture to a heavy-duty resealable plastic bag; cut a small hole in a corner of bag.

4. Gently squeeze the filling into the cavity of each cupcake until you feel a slight resistance. Brush any remaining milk mixture over tops of the cupcakes. Cover and refrigerate 4 hours or overnight. Top with the whipped cream and fruit. Store in the refrigerator.

FAST FIX ▸ COWABUNGA ROOT BEER CUPCAKES

I developed these cupcakes for my daughter's first birthday and transported them using dry ice. Be careful not to freeze them solid!

—MINDY CARSWELL WALKER, MI

PREP: 10 MIN. • **BAKE:** 15 MIN. + COOLING • **MAKES:** 24 SERVINGS

- 1 **package butter recipe golden cake mix (regular size)**
- 4 **teaspoons root beer concentrate, divided**
- 1 **carton (12 ounces) frozen whipped topping, thawed**
  Vanilla ice cream

1. Prepare and bake the cupcakes according to package directions, adding 2 teaspoons root beer concentrate when mixing batter. Remove to wire racks to cool completely.

2. In a small bowl, mix whipped topping and remaining root beer concentrate until blended; spread over the cupcakes. Serve with ice cream.

NOTE *This recipe was tested with McCormick root beer concentrate.*

SUNSHINE CUPCAKES

Cute, easy and fun, these cheery lemon cupcakes will bring lots of smiles.

—TASTE OF HOME TEST KITCHEN

PREP: 20 MIN.
BAKE: 20 MIN. + COOLING
MAKE: 2 DOZEN

- **1 package lemon cake mix (regular size)**
- **1 can (16 ounces) vanilla frosting**
   Yellow food coloring
   Miniature semisweet chocolate chips, red shoestring licorice and candy corn

1. Prepare and bake cake batter according to package directions for cupcakes. Cool completely.

2. In a small bowl, tint frosting yellow. Frost cupcakes. Press two chocolate chips into each cupcake for eyes. For mouths, cut licorice into 1-in. pieces; bent slightly to curve. Press one licorice piece into each cupcake. Add candy corn around edges of cupcakes.

CHIP LOVER'S CUPCAKES

Making chocolate chip cookies is a challenge with three teenagers who are always grabbing a sample of the dough. Their cookie dough cravings inspired the recipe for these cupcakes that adults will enjoy, too.

—DONNA SCULLY MIDDLETOWN, DE

PREP: 30 MIN. • **BAKE:** 20 MIN. + COOLING • **MAKES:** 1½ DOZEN

1 **package white cake mix (regular size)**
¼ **cup butter, softened**
¼ **cup packed brown sugar**
2 **tablespoons sugar**
⅓ **cup all-purpose flour**
¼ **cup confectioners' sugar**
¼ **cup miniature semisweet chocolate chips**

BUTTERCREAM FROSTING
½ **cup butter, softened**
½ **cup shortening**
4½ **cups confectioners' sugar**
4 **tablespoons 2% milk, divided**
1½ **teaspoons vanilla extract**
¼ **cup baking cocoa**
18 **miniature chocolate chip cookies**

1. Prepare cake batter according to package directions; set aside. For filling, in a small bowl, cream butter and sugars until light and fluffy. Gradually beat in the flour and confectioners' sugar until blended. Fold in chocolate chips.

2. Fill paper-lined muffin cups half full with cake batter. Drop filling by tablespoonfuls into the center of each; cover with the remaining batter.

3. Bake at 350° for 20-22 minutes or until a toothpick inserted in cake comes out clean. Cool for 10 minutes before removing from the pans to wire racks to cool completely.

4. For frosting, in a large bowl, cream the butter, shortening and confectioners' sugar until smooth. Beat in 3 tablespoons milk and vanilla until creamy. Set aside 1 cup frosting; frost cupcakes with the remaining frosting.

5. Stir the baking cocoa and remaining milk into reserved frosting. Cut a small hole in a corner of a pastry or plastic bag; insert star tip. Fill bag with the chocolate frosting. Pipe a rosette on top of each cupcake; garnish with a cookie.

CHERRY CORDIAL CAKE BALLS

Brandy and coffee add mild flavor to these scrumptious cherry cake balls.

—SUSAN WESTERFIELD ALBUQUERQUE, NM

PREP: 1 HOUR • **BAKE:** 35 MIN. + STANDING • **MAKES:** 6 DOZEN

- 1 **package fudge marble cake mix (regular size)**
- 1¼ **cups plus 3 tablespoons strong brewed coffee, divided**
- ¼ **cup canola oil**
- 3 **eggs**
- 1 **jar (10 ounces) maraschino cherries without stems, well drained**
- ⅓ **cup brandy**
- ¼ **cup cherry preserves**
- 1 **cup canned chocolate frosting**
- 4 **pounds milk chocolate candy coating, chopped**
- 2 **tablespoons shortening**

1. In a large bowl, combine the cake mix, 1¼ cups coffee, oil and eggs; beat on low speed for 30 seconds. Beat on medium for 2 minutes. Pour batter into a greased and floured 13x9-in. baking pan.

2. Bake at 350° for 30-35 minutes or until a toothpick inserted near the center comes out clean. Cool completely.

3. Place cherries in a food processor; cover and process until coarsely chopped. Transfer to a small bowl; stir in the brandy, preserves and remaining coffee.

4. Crumble cake into a large bowl. Add the frosting and cherry mixture; beat well. Shape into 1-in. balls.

5. In a microwave, melt candy coating and shortening; stir until smooth. Dip balls in chocolate mixture; allow excess to drip off. Place on waxed paper; let stand until set. Store in an airtight container overnight before serving.

PATRIOTIC ICE CREAM CUPCAKES

Create flavor fireworks with these ice cream cupcakes. The hand-held treats feature red velvet cake, blue moon ice cream and creamy, white frozen topping.
—TASTE OF HOME TEST KITCHEN

PREP: 30 MIN. + FREEZING
BAKE: 15 MIN. + COOLING
MAKES: 3 DOZEN

- 1 **package red velvet cake mix (regular size)**
- 1 **quart blue moon ice cream, softened**
- 3 **cups heavy whipping cream**
- 1½ **cups marshmallow creme**
  Red, white and blue sprinkles
  Blue colored sugar

1. Prepare the cake mix batter according to package directions for cupcakes.

2. Fill paper-lined muffin cups half full. Bake at 350° for 11-14 minutes or until a toothpick inserted near the center comes out clean. Cool for 10 minutes before removing from pans to wire racks to cool completely.

3. Working quickly, spread ice cream over cupcakes. Freeze for at least 1 hour.

4. In a large bowl, combine the cream and marshmallow creme; beat until stiff peaks form. Pipe over cupcakes; decorate with sprinkles and colored sugar. Freeze for 4 hours or until firm.

NOTE *As a substitute for blue moon ice cream, tint softened vanilla ice cream with blue food coloring.*

SCAREDY-CAT CUPCAKES

Get your kids in on the fun by letting them add the faces to these feline cupcakes.
Adults can pipe on the frosting while the kids decorate.

—TASTE OF HOME TEST KITCHEN

PREP: 1 HOUR • **BAKE:** 20 MIN. + COOLING • **MAKES:** 2 DOZEN

 1   **package cake mix of your choice (regular size)**
 1   **can (16 ounces) vanilla frosting**
     Orange paste food coloring
 1   **cup chow mein noodles**
 2   **teaspoons sugar**
 2   **teaspoons baking cocoa**
48   **nacho tortilla chips, broken**
     Assorted candies: green M&M's, miniature semisweet chocolate chips, black licorice twists and shoestring licorice

1. Prepare and bake cake mix according to package directions for cupcakes; cool completely.

2. Tint vanilla frosting orange. Using a star tip, pipe the orange frosting onto cupcakes.

3. For whiskers, in a small bowl, combine the chow mein noodles, sugar and cocoa; set aside.

4. For cats' ears, insert nacho chips with pointed tips up. Use M&M's and miniature chocolate chips for eyes, pieces of licorice twists for noses and shoestring licorice for mouths. Arrange reserved chow mein noodles on cupcakes for whiskers.

CANNOLI CUPCAKES

These jumbo cupcakes feature a fluffy cannoli-like filling. White chocolate curls on top are the crowning touch.

—TASTE OF HOME TEST KITCHEN

PREP: 50 MIN. • **BAKE:** 25 MIN. + COOLING • **MAKES:** 8 CUPCAKES

- **1 package white cake mix (regular size)**
- **¾ cup heavy whipping cream, divided**
- **1 cup ricotta cheese**
- **1 cup confectioners' sugar**
- **½ cup mascarpone cheese**
- **¼ teaspoon almond extract**
- **½ cup chopped pistachios**
- **4 ounces white baking chocolate, chopped**
  White chocolate curls

1. Prepare the cake mix batter according to package directions. Fill paper-lined jumbo muffin cups three-fourths full.

2. Bake according to package directions for 24-28 minutes or until a toothpick inserted near the center comes out clean. Cool for 10 minutes before removing from the pans to wire racks to cool completely.

3. In a small bowl, beat ½ cup cream until stiff peaks form; set aside. In a large bowl, combine ricotta cheese, confectioner's sugar, mascarpone cheese and extract until smooth. Fold in pistachios and whipped cream.

4. Cut tops off of each cupcake. Spread or pipe cupcakes with the cheese mixture; replace the tops.

5. In a small saucepan, melt white baking chocolate with the remaining cream over low heat; stir until smooth. Remove from heat. Cool to room temperature. Spoon over cupcakes; sprinkle with chocolate curls. Store in the refrigerator.

CARAMEL CASHEW CAKE POPS

Nothing beats the pairing of buttery caramel and rich cashews;
add it to a chocolaty cake pop and you have one irresistible little treat.

—TASTE OF HOME TEST KITCHEN

PREP: 1½ HOURS + CHILLING • **MAKES:** 4 DOZEN

1 **package chocolate cake mix (regular size)**
¾ **cup canned dulce de leche**
48 **lollipop sticks**
2½ **pounds milk chocolate candy coating, coarsely chopped**
 Chopped cashews

1. Prepare and bake cake mix according to package directions, using a greased 13-in. x 9-in. baking pan. Cool completely on a wire rack.

2. Crumble cake into a large bowl. Add dulce de leche and mix well. Shape into 1-in. balls. Place on baking sheets; insert sticks.

Freeze for at least 2 hours or refrigerate for at least 3 hours or until cake balls are firm.

3. In a microwave, melt candy coating. Dip each cake ball in coating; allow excess to drip off. Coat with cashews. Insert cake pops into a plastic foam block to stand. Let stand until set.

TRUFFLE CHOCOLATE CUPCAKES

I enjoy food with an unexpected twist, like these cupcakes with a creamy chocolate truffle center.
My kids love to help make them, but I have to be sure to have enough truffles saved to actually fill the cupcakes!

—AMANDA NOLL SPANAWAY, WA

PREP: 40 MIN. + CHILLING • **BAKE:** 20 MIN. + COOLING • **MAKES:** 2 DOZEN

1½ cups semisweet chocolate
chips
½ cup plus 2 tablespoons
sweetened condensed milk
1 teaspoon butter
2 teaspoons vanilla extract

CUPCAKES
1 package devil's food cake mix
(regular size)
4 eggs
1 cup (8 ounces) sour cream
¾ cup canola oil
½ cup water
2 teaspoons vanilla extract
1 cup heavy whipping cream,
whipped, optional

1. For truffles, in a small saucepan, melt chocolate, milk and butter over low heat; stir until blended. Remove from the heat. Stir in vanilla. Transfer to a small bowl; cover and chill until firm, about 1 hour. Roll into twenty-four 1-in. balls; chill 1 hour longer.

2. For cupcakes, in a large bowl, combine the cake mix, eggs. sour cream, oil, water and vanilla; beat on low speed for 30 seconds. Beat on medium for 2 minutes.

3. Fill paper-lined muffin cups one-third full. Drop a truffle into center of each cupcake. Top with remaining batter. Bake at 350° for 17-22 minutes or until a toothpick inserted comes out clean.

4. Cool for 10 minutes before removing from pans to wire racks to cool completely. Top with whipped cream if desired.

CLOWN CUPCAKES

Throwing a children's party can be a real circus if you serve these colorful clown cupcakes. Set up a cupcake decorating table and let the kids make funny faces with their favorite candies.

—TASTE OF HOME TEST KITCHEN

PREP: 2 HOURS
BAKE: 20 MIN. + COOLINGS
MAKES: 2 DOZEN

- 1 **package yellow cake mix (regular size)**
- 3 **cans (16 ounces each) vanilla frosting, divided**
  Yellow, red and blue paste food coloring
- 24 **ice cream sugar cones**
  Assorted candies: M&M's miniature baking bits, red shoestring licorice and cherry sour ball candies

1. Prepare and bake cake batter according to package directions for cupcakes. Cool completely. Divide two cans of frosting among three bowls; tint with yellow, red and blue food coloring.
2. For clown hats, use a serrated knife or kitchen scissors to cut 2 in. from the open end of each cone. Frost cones with tinted frosting; decorate with baking bits. Place on waxed paper for 30 minutes or until frosting is set.
3. Frost cupcakes with remaining vanilla frosting. Leaving room for the hat on each cupcake, make a clown face and hair with candies. Pipe a matching ruffle on each. Carefully position a hat on each cupcake; pipe ruffle around bottom..

COCONUT-ALMOND FUDGE CUPS

With a coconut filling, the flavor of these fudgy bites is reminiscent of an Almond Joy candy bar.
The recipe makes a big batch, and they make thoughtful party favors for a take-home treat.
—PRECI D'SILVA DALLAS, TX

PREP: 30 MIN. • **BAKE:** 10 MIN./BATCH + COOLING • **MAKES:** 4 DOZEN

1 **package chocolate fudge cake mix (regular size)**
½ **cup butter, melted**
1 **egg**

FILLING
¼ **cup sugar**
¼ **cup evaporated milk**
7 **large marshmallows**
1 **cup flaked coconut**

TOPPING
¾ **cup semisweet chocolate chips**
¼ **cup evaporated milk**
2 **tablespoons butter**
½ **cup sliced almonds**

1. In a large bowl, beat the cake mix, butter and egg until well blended. Shape into 1-in. balls; place in foil-lined miniature muffin cups. Bake at 350° for 8 minutes.

2. Using the end of a wooden spoon handle, make a ½-in.-deep indentation in the center of each cup. Bake 2-3 minutes longer or until cake springs back when lightly touched. Remove from pans to wire racks to cool.

3. For filling, in a microwave-safe bowl, heat sugar and milk on high for 2 minutes, stirring frequently. Add marshmallows; stir until melted. Stir in coconut. Spoon into cooled cups.

4. For topping, in another microwave-safe bowl, combine the chocolate chips, milk and butter. Microwave in 10- to 20-second intervals until melted; stir until smooth. Stir in almonds. Spread over filling. Store in the refrigerator.

NOTE *This recipe was tested in a 1,100-watt microwave.*

CHOCOLATE FROSTED PEANUT BUTTER CUPCAKES

Cupcakes are for everyone! My dad and brothers love peanut butter cups which are the inspiration for these goodies.

—ALISA CHRISTENSEN RANCHO SANTA MARGARITA, CA

PREP: 30 MIN. • **BAKE:** 20 MIN. + COOLING • **MAKES:** 2 DOZEN

- **1 package yellow cake mix (regular size)**
- **¾ cup creamy peanut butter**
- **3 eggs**
- **1¼ cups water**
- **¼ cup canola oil**

FROSTING

- **1⅔ cups semisweet chocolate chips**
- **½ cup heavy whipping cream**
- **½ cup butter, softened**
- **1 cup confectioners' sugar**

1. In a large bowl, combine the cake mix, peanut butter, eggs, water and oil; beat on low speed for 30 seconds. Beat on medium for 2 minutes. Fill paper-lined muffin cups two-thirds full.

2. Bake at 350° for 18-22 minutes or until a toothpick inserted near the center comes out clean. Cool for 10 minutes before removing from the pans to wire racks to cool completely.

3. Place chocolate chips in a large bowl. In a small saucepan, bring cream just to a boil. Pour over chocolate; whisk until smooth. Cool, stirring occasionally, to room temperature. Add butter and confectioners' sugar; beat until smooth. Frost cupcakes.
NOTE *Reduced-fat peanut butter is not recommended for this recipe.*

FARM FRIEND CUPCAKES

These chick, pig and moo-cow cupcakes can't get cuter. Pick a favorite animal and prepare to delight your little ones!

—COLLEEN PALMER EPPING, NH

PREP: 45 MIN. • **BAKE:** 25 MIN. + COOLING • **MAKES:** 2 DOZEN

- **1 package devil's food cake mix (regular size)**

FOR PIGS
- **1 can (16 ounces) vanilla frosting**
- **Pink paste food coloring**

FOR CHICKS
- **1 to 2 cans (16 ounces each) vanilla frosting**
- **Yellow paste food coloring**

FOR MOO-COWS
- **1 can (16 ounces) vanilla frosting**
- **Pink paste food coloring**
- **1 can (16 ounces) chocolate frosting**

FOR FACES
- **Miniature semisweet chocolate chips**
- **Semisweet chocolate chips**
- **Halved miniature marshmallows**
- **Assorted candies (Brach's white dessert mints, pink mint candy lozenges, Good & Plenty candies and candy corn)**

1. Prepare cake batter according to package directions. Fill 24 paper-lined muffin cups two-thirds full. Bake at 350° for 21-26 minutes or until a toothpick inserted near the center comes out clean. Cool for 10 minutes before removing from pans to wire racks. Cool completely.

2. *For pigs*, tint frosting pink; frost cupcakes. Attach miniature chocolate chips and dessert mints for eyes, pink candy lozenges for snouts, miniature chocolate chips for nostrils and Good & Plenty candies for ears.

3. *For chicks*, tint frosting yellow. Insert #17 star tip in a pastry bag. Transfer frosting to bag; pipe stars to cover top of cupcakes. Pipe a large ball for heads. Pipe on wings using a leaf tip. Attach miniature chocolate chips and dessert mints for eyes and candy corn for beaks.

4. *For moo-cows*, tint ¼ cup vanilla frosting pink, set aside. With remaining white frosting, create a white face-shaped stripe down the center of each cupcake. Fill in the unfrosted portion with the chocolate frosting. Attach the chocolate chips for eyes, the miniature chips for noses and marshmallow halves for ears. With reserved pink frosting, create mouths and fill in ears.

FAST FIX ▸ CARROT-TOPPED CUPCAKES

A handy spice cake mix becomes fabulous carrot cupcakes with shredded carrots and chopped walnuts. The minicakes are eye-catching, too, when decorated with carrots piped on with prepared cream cheese frosting and parsley sprigs for the green tops.
—TASTE OF HOME TEST KITCHEN

PREP: 15 MIN. • **BAKE:** 20 MIN.
MAKES: 2 DOZEN

- 1 **package spice cake mix (regular size)**
- 1½ **cups shredded carrots**
- ½ **cup chopped walnuts**
- 1 **teaspoon ground cinnamon**
- 1 **can (16 ounces) cream cheese frosting**
  Orange paste food coloring
  Fresh parsley sprigs

1. Prepare cake batter according to the package directions. Fold in carrots, walnuts and cinnamon. Fill paper-lined muffin cups half full.

2. Bake at 350° for 18-23 minutes or until a toothpick inserted near center comes out clean. Remove from the pans to wire racks to cool completely.

3. Frost cupcakes with 1¼ cups frosting. Place remaining frosting in a small resealable bag; tint with orange food coloring. Cut a small hole in the corner of bag; pipe a carrot on the top of each cupcake. Add a parsley sprig for greens.

RAISIN-ZUCCHINI SPICE CUPCAKES

We were out of flour one night when I wanted to make zucchini muffins,
so I used a package of spice cake mix instead. They were a huge hit with the kids and my husband.

—TRACY SCHERER CLIMAX, MI

PREP: 30 MIN. • **BAKE:** 20 MIN. + COOLING • **MAKES:** 2 DOZEN

- **1 package spice cake mix (regular size)**
- **1⅓ cups water**
- **¼ cup canola oil**
- **3 eggs**
- **2 cups shredded zucchini**
- **½ cup raisins**

CINNAMON FROSTING

- **¼ cup butter, softened**
- **1¾ cups confectioners' sugar**
- **1 teaspoon vanilla extract**
- **½ teaspoon ground cinnamon**
- **⅛ teaspoon ground nutmeg**
- **1 to 2 tablespoons 2% milk**

1. In a large bowl, combine the cake mix, water, oil and eggs; beat on low speed for 30 seconds. Beat on medium for 2 minutes. Stir in zucchini and raisins. Fill paper-lined muffin cups two-thirds full.

2. Bake at 350° for 18-22 minutes or until a toothpick inserted near the center comes out clean. Cool for 10 minutes before removing to wire racks to cool completely.

3. For frosting, in a small bowl, beat butter until light and fluffy. Beat in the confectioners' sugar, vanilla, cinnamon, nutmeg and enough milk to reach a spreading consistency. Frost cupcakes.

CREAM CHEESE CUPCAKES

It's hard to believe these cupcakes can taste so delicious and be so easy.
Frost them if you wish, but my family likes them plain, which is
great when I'm having an especially busy day.

—**NANCY REICHERT** THOMASVILLE, GA

PREP: 10 MIN. • **BAKE:** 25 MIN. • **MAKES:** 2 DOZEN

1 **package (3 ounces) cream cheese, softened**
1 **package yellow cake mix (regular size)**
1¼ **cups water**
½ **cup butter, melted**
3 **eggs**
   Chocolate frosting, optional

1. In a large bowl, beat the cream cheese until smooth. Beat in the cake mix, water, butter and eggs. Spoon batter by ¼ cupfuls into paper-lined muffin cups.
2. Bake at 350° for 25 minutes or until golden brown. Remove to a wire rack to cool completely. Frost if desired.

MONKEY CUPCAKES

These never fail to make my kids smile, and they're always a hit at bake sales.

—**SANDRA SEAMAN** GREENSBURG, PA

PREP: 30 MIN. • **BAKE:** 20 MIN. + COOLING • **MAKES:** 2 DOZEN

1 **package chocolate cake mix (regular size)**
1 **can (16 ounces) chocolate frosting**
24 **vanilla wafers**
   Black and red decorating gel
48 **pastel blue and/or green milk chocolate M&M's**
12 **Nutter Butter cookies**

1. Prepare cake batter and bake according to package directions for cupcakes; cool completely.
2. Set aside ¼ cup frosting. Frost cupcakes with the remaining frosting. With a serrated knife, cut off and discard a fourth of each vanilla wafer. Place a wafer on each cupcake, with the rounded edge of wafer near edge of cupcake, for face. Add dots of black gel for nostrils. With red gel, pipe on mouths.

3. Place M&M's above wafers for eyes; add dots of black gel for pupils. Using reserved frosting and a #16 star tip, pipe hair. Carefully separate cookies; cut each in half. Position one on each side of cupcakes for ears.
HOW-TO *Kids' little fingers are just the right size for placing pieces. Give kids creative freedom to ensure that no two monkey faces are the same.*

CLEMENTINE CUPCAKES

Have your cupcake and eat it, too! Clementines give these cupcakes
a fresh, fancy feel that's sure to please most palates.

—TASTE OF HOME TEST KITCHEN

PREP: 25 MIN. • **BAKE:** 15 MIN. + COOLING • **MAKES:** 2 DOZEN

- **1 package white cake mix (regular size)**
- **¾ cup water**
- **4 egg whites**
- **½ cup clementine juice (about 5 clementines)**
- **¼ cup canola oil**
- **1 teaspoon grated clementine peel**
- **4 clementines, peeled, sectioned and membrane removed**

FROSTING
- **⅓ cup butter, softened**
- **3 cups confectioners' sugar**
- **½ teaspoon grated clementine peel**
- **5 to 6 teaspoons clementine juice**

GARNISH
- **¾ cup semisweet chocolate chips**
- **24 clementine sections with membrane (about 2½ clementines)**

1. In a large bowl, combine the first six ingredients; beat on low speed for 30 seconds. Beat on medium for 2 minutes. Fill paper-lined muffin cups half full. Place one clementine section in the center of each; gently press down into batter. Chop remaining sections; sprinkle over batter.

2. Bake at 350° for 15-20 minutes or until a toothpick inserted near the center comes out clean. Cool for 10 minutes before removing from the pans to wire racks to cool completely.

3. For frosting, in a small bowl, beat butter until light and fluffy. Beat in the confectioners' sugar, clementine peel and enough juice to reach spreading consistency. Frost cupcakes.

4. In a small microwave-safe bowl, melt chocolate chips; stir until smooth. Dip clementine sections halfway into chocolate; allow excess to drip off. Place on a waxed paper-lined baking sheet; refrigerate until set. Place one on each cupcake.

PUMPKIN STREUSEL CUPCAKES

A delicious crumb filling becomes the center of attention inside these yummy confections that taste like pumpkin bread.

—DONNA GISH BLUE SPRINGS, MO

PREP: 25 MIN. • **BAKE:** 20 MIN. + COOLING • **MAKES:** 2 DOZEN

1 package spice cake mix (regular size)
1¼ cups water
3 eggs
½ cup canned pumpkin
STREUSEL
½ cup packed brown sugar
½ teaspoon ground cinnamon
1 tablespoon butter
FROSTING
1 package (8 ounces) cream cheese, softened
2 tablespoons butter
2 cups confectioners' sugar
½ teaspoon vanilla extract

1. In a large bowl, combine cake mix, water, eggs and pumpkin. Beat on low speed just until moistened. Beat on medium for 2 minutes.

2. In a small bowl, combine brown sugar and cinnamon; cut in butter until crumbly. Fill paper-lined muffin cups one-fourth full with batter. Drop streusel by heaping teaspoonfuls into center of each cupcake. Cover with remaining batter.

3. Bake at 350° for 18-20 minutes or until a toothpick inserted in the cake portion comes out clean. Cool for 10 minutes before removing from the pans to wire racks to cool completely.

4. In a small bowl, beat the cream cheese and butter until fluffy. Add confectioners' sugar and vanilla; beat until smooth. Frost cupcakes. Store in the refrigerator.

CARAMEL APPLE CUPCAKES

Bring these extra-special cupcakes to your next event and watch how quickly they disappear! Kids will go for the fun appearance and tasty toppings, while adults will appreciate the tender spiced cake underneath.

—DIANE HALFERTY CORPUS CHRISTI, TX

PREP: 25 MIN.
BAKE: 20 MIN. + COOLING
MAKES: 1 DOZEN

- 1 **package spice or carrot cake mix (regular size)**
- 2 **cups chopped peeled tart apples**
- 20 **caramels**
- 3 **tablespoons 2% milk**
- 1 **cup finely chopped pecans, toasted**
- 12 **Popsicle sticks**

1. Prepare cake batter according to the package directions; fold in the apples.

2. Fill 12 greased or paper-lined jumbo muffin cups three-fourths full. Bake at 350° for 20 minutes or until a toothpick inserted near the center comes out clean. Cool for 10 minutes before removing from the pans to wire racks to cool completely.

3. In a small saucepan, melt the caramels with milk over low heat until smooth. Spread over the cupcakes. Sprinkle with pecans. Insert a wooden stick into the center of each cupcake.

FRUIT-FILLED CUPCAKES

Kids really love the fruity surprise tucked inside these sweet, pretty pink cupcakes.

—MARGARET WILSON SUN CITY, CA

PREP: 30 MIN. • **BAKE:** 25 MIN. + COOLING • **MAKES:** ABOUT 2 DOZEN

1 **package strawberry cake mix (regular size)**
2 **cups (16 ounces) sour cream**
2 **eggs**
⅓ **cup strawberry preserves**
1 **can (16 ounces) vanilla frosting, divided**
  Red food coloring, optional
  Red nonpareils and pink jimmies, optional

1. In a large bowl, combine the cake mix, sour cream and eggs. Beat on low speed for 30 seconds; beat on medium for 2 minutes.
2. Fill 27 paper-lined muffin cups half full. Using the end of a wooden spoon handle, make an indentation in the center of each; fill with ½ teaspoon preserves. Top with remaining batter.
3. Bake at 350° for 22-27 minutes or until a toothpick inserted in the cake portion comes out clean. Cool for 10 minutes before removing from pans to wire racks to cool completely.
4. If desired, place a third of the frosting in a small bowl; tint pink with red food coloring. Frost cupcakes with white frosting; if desired, pipe edges with pink frosting. Decorate with the nonpareils and jimmies if desired.

FAST FIX ▶ CUPCAKES WITH PEANUT BUTTER FROSTING

My family just loves these cupcakes, especially the subtle taste of peanut butter in the frosting. Chocolate frosting is equally delicious on top.
—ALYCE WYMAN PEMBINA, ND

PREP: 15 MIN. • **BAKE:** 20 MIN. + COOLING • **MAKES:** 1½ DOZEN

- **1 package white cake mix (regular size)**
- **18 miniature peanut butter cups**
- **1⅓ cups prepared vanilla frosting**
- **2 tablespoons creamy peanut butter**

1. Prepare cake mix according to package directions. Spoon about 2 tablespoons of batter into each paper-lined muffin cup. Place a peanut butter cup in each; fill two-thirds full with remaining batter.

2. Bake at 350° for 20-25 minutes or until lightly browned and a toothpick inserted in the cake portion comes out clean. Cool for 10 minutes before removing from the pans to wire racks to cool completely.

3. In a small bowl, combine frosting and peanut butter until smooth. Frost cupcakes.

CUPCAKE CONES

I experimented with these cupcakes when my girls were young. Now, I'm a grandmother of nine, and these are still our favorites. They're a great treat for kids to take to school.
—BETTY ANDERSON STURGEON BAY, WI

PREP: 25 MIN. • **BAKE:** 25 MIN. • **MAKES:** ABOUT 3 DOZEN

- **1 package chocolate cake mix (regular size)**
- **1 package (8 ounces) cream cheese, softened**
- **⅓ cup sugar**
- **1 egg**
- **½ teaspoon vanilla extract**
- **1 cup miniature semisweet chocolate chips**
- **36 ice-cream cake cones (about 3 inches tall)**

FROSTING
- **½ cup shortening**
- **3¾ cups confectioners' sugar**
- **1 teaspoon vanilla extract**
- **4 to 5 tablespoons milk**
  Sprinkles

1. Prepare cake mix according to package directions; set aside. In a large bowl, beat the cream cheese, sugar, egg and vanilla until smooth; stir in chocolate chips.

2. Place ice-cream cones in muffin cups. Spoon about 1 tablespoon of cake batter into each cone; top with a rounded teaspoon of cream cheese mixture. Fill with remaining batter to within ¾ inch of top.

3. Bake at 350° for 25-30 minutes or until a toothpick inserted in cake comes out clean. Cool completely.

4. In a small bowl, beat the shortening, confectioners' sugar and vanilla until smooth. Add enough milk to reach spreading consistency. Frost tops of cooled cones and top with sprinkles.
NOTE *These cupcakes are best served the day they are made.*

CARAMEL APPLE CAKE POPS

For a perfect fall treat, mix spice cake and apples with frosting to form cake balls.
Then dip them in caramel coating and let the kids go nuts, rolling them in peanuts.
—TASTE OF HOME TEST KITCHEN

PREP: 1 HOUR + FREEZING • **BAKE:** 25 MIN. + COOLING • **MAKES:** 39 CAKE POPS

- 1 **package spice cake mix (regular size)**
- 1½ **cups finely chopped peeled tart apples**
- ¼ **cup packed brown sugar**
- 2 **tablespoons plus 2 teaspoons heavy whipping cream**
- 2 **tablespoons butter**
- ½ **cup confectioners' sugar**
- 2 **packages (11 ounces each) Kraft caramel bits**
- ¼ **cup water**
- 39 **lollipop sticks**
- 1 **cup finely chopped salted peanuts**

1. Prepare the cake mix batter according to package directions, adding the apples after mixing. Pour into two greased and floured 9-in. round baking pans. Bake according to package directions. Cool completely.

2. In a small saucepan, combine brown sugar, cream and butter. Bring to a boil over medium heat, stirring constantly. Remove from the heat; cool for 5 minutes. Gradually beat in confectioners' sugar until smooth.

3. Crumble one cake layer into a large bowl. (Save remaining cake for another use.) Add brown sugar mixture; mix well. Shape into 1-in. balls. Arrange on waxed paper-lined baking sheets. Freeze for at least 2 hours or until firm.

4. In a large saucepan, combine caramel bits and water. Cook and stir over medium-low heat until smooth. Dip ends of the lollipop sticks into caramel and insert into cake balls. Dip balls in caramel; roll bottoms in peanuts. Let stand until set. Store in an airtight container in the refrigerator.

THE GREAT PUMPKIN CAKES

These are the ultimate confectionery tribute to Charlie Brown's Great Pumpkin. The little round cakes are surprisingly easy to make—just put two cupcakes together, frost and decorate with vines and leaves.

—SHARON SKILDUM MAPLE GROVE, MN

PREP: 50 MIN. • **BAKE:** 15 MIN. + COOLING • **MAKES:** 1 DOZEN

- **1 package yellow cake mix or cake mix of your choice (regular size)**
- **2 cans (16 ounces each) vanilla frosting, divided**
- **1 to 1½ teaspoons orange paste food coloring**
- **12 green gumdrops**
- **½ teaspoon green paste food coloring**

1. Prepare the cake batter according to package directions. Fill 24 greased muffin cups two-thirds full. Bake at 350° for 15-18 minutes or until a toothpick inserted in center comes out clean. Cool for 5 minutes before removing from the pans to wire racks to cool completely.

2. For frosting, in a small bowl, combine 1½ cans frosting; tint orange. Cut a thin slice off the top of each cupcake. Spread frosting on 12 cupcakes. Invert remaining cupcakes and place on top; frost top and sides.

3. For stems, place one gumdrop on each pumpkin. Tint remaining frosting green. Cut a small hole in the corner of a pastry or plastic bag; insert #5 round tip and fill with a third of the green frosting. Pipe curly vines from pumpkin stems. Using green frosting and #352 leaf tip, pipe leaves randomly along the vines.

FAST FIX ▸ CHOCOLATE CHERRY CUPCAKES

Inside each of these cupcakes is a fruity surprise! Chocolate and cherries are such a fabulous combo that both kids and adults will love them.

—BERTILLE COOPER CALIFORNIA, MD

PREP: 15 MIN. • **BAKE:** 20 MIN. • **MAKES:** 2 DOZEN

1 **package chocolate cake mix (regular size)**
1⅓ **cups water**
½ **cup canola oil**
3 **eggs**
1 **can (21 ounces) cherry pie filling**
1 **can (16 ounces) vanilla frosting**
Chocolate curls, optional

1. In a large bowl, combine the cake mix, water, oil and eggs; beat on low speed for 30 seconds. Beat on medium for 2 minutes.

2. Spoon batter by ¼ cupfuls into paper-lined muffin cups. Place a rounded teaspoonful of pie filling in the center of each cupcake. Set remaining pie filling aside.

3. Bake at 350° for 20-25 minutes or until a toothpick inserted near the center comes out clean. Cool 10 minutes; remove from pans to wire racks to cool completely.

4. Frost cupcakes; top each with one cherry from pie filling. Refrigerate remaining pie filling for another use. Garnish with chocolate curls if desired.

{3}

Party Cakes

80

Colorful Easter Cake

88

Black Forest Cake

98

Circus Cake

COLORFUL EASTER CAKE

Jelly beans and Fruit Roll-Ups offer a fun, festive touch to your creation.

—TASTE OF HOME TEST KITCHEN

PREP: 30 MIN. • **BAKE:** 25 MIN. + COOLING • **MAKES:** 12 SERVINGS

1 **package white cake mix (regular size)**

1 **can (16 ounces) vanilla frosting**

Fruit Roll-Ups

Jelly beans

Decorating icing of your choice

1. Prepare and bake the cake according to package directions, using two greased 9-in. round baking pans. Cool for 10 minutes before removing from pans to wire racks to cool completely.

2. Spread frosting between layers and over top and sides of cake.

3. Cut Fruit Roll-Ups into strips of desired widths. Lightly press onto sides of cake. Arrange jelly beans around edges of cake. Decorate with icing as desired.

HOW-TO *Before writing on the cake with icing, lightly outline the words with a toothpick.*

FRANKIE'S BRIDE CAKE

Let his hair-raising cake be the star of your next Halloween party.
Because she's made with a convenient cake mix, you'll have plenty of time to decorate her BOOtifully!
—TASTE OF HOME TEST KITCHEN

PREP: 1¼ HOURS • **BAKE:** 35 MIN. + COOLING • **MAKES:** 16-20 SERVINGS

1 **package yellow cake mix (regular size)**
1 **cup butter, softened**
1 **cup shortening**
7½ **to 8 cups confectioners' sugar**
¼ **cup milk**
3 **teaspoons vanilla extract**
⅛ **teaspoon salt**
Purple and green paste food coloring
ASSORTED CANDIES: Large marshmallow, black raspberry candies, black shoestring licorice, green Jordan almond, red shoestring licorice, red colored sugar, red raspberry candy, green sour gummy stars, candy corn, large black spice gumdrops and black licorice pastels

1. Prepare cake mix according to package directions. Pour batter into two greased and floured 9-in. x 5-in. loaf pans.

2. Bake at 350° for 35-40 minutes or until a toothpick inserted near the center comes out clean. Cool for 10 minutes before removing from pans to wire racks to cool. Place cakes end-to-end on a 22-in. x 8-in. covered board.

3. In a large bowl, cream butter and shortening until light and fluffy. Beat in 6 cups of the confectioners' sugar, milk, vanilla and salt. Beat in enough of the remaining confectioners' sugar to reach spreading consistency. Set aside ¼ cup white frosting for hair. Remove 3 cups frosting; tint purple. Tint remaining frosting green.

4. For bride's face, frost the top and sides of one cake with green frosting. Frost the second cake with a thin layer of purple frosting. Insert a medium star tip in each of two pastry bags; fill one bag with the remaining purple frosting and the other with the reserved white frosting. Pipe wavy purple hair with streaks of wavy white hair on bride.

5. Decorate the bride, using assorted candies. For eyes, use halved marshmallow, halved black raspberry candy and black shoestring licorice. Add a Jordan almond nose. Make a smiling mouth and dimples using the red shoestring licorice, red colored sugar and halved red raspberry candy.

6. For ears and earrings, insert gummy stars and candy corn into side of cake. Attach the spice gumdrops for bolts. Use the black shoestring licorice and black licorice pastels for the scar. Add a spider made with a black raspberry candy and black shoestring licorice strips.

RACETRACK CAKE

Everyone gets fired up when they see my Racetrack Cake. Miniature racecars look so cute speeding around the bend.

—**AMBER KIMMICH** POWHATAN, VA

PREP: 3 HOURS • **BAKE:** 30 MIN. + COOLING • **MAKES:** 24-30 SERVINGS

- **1 package white cake mix (regular size)**
- **1 package chocolate cake mix (regular size)**
- **10 cups buttercream frosting**
  Black, yellow and red food coloring
  Green edible glitter
- **4 miniature cars**
- **2 miniature checkered flags**

1. Prepare and bake each cake according to package directions, using greased 13-in. x 9-in. baking pans. Cool for 10 minutes before inverting onto wire racks to cool completely.

2. Transfer cakes to a covered board and position side-by-side. Frost top of cakes with 5⅓ cups of frosting. Tint 1½ cups frosting black. Cut a small hole in the corner of a pastry or plastic bag; fill with black frosting. Outline edge of cake. Using a #17 star tip, pipe a checkered pattern on sides of cake with 1 cup white frosting and remaining black frosting.

3. Tint ⅔ cup frosting gray; create an oval racetrack in middle of cake. Tint ¾ cup frosting yellow; pipe lines around track and infield. For grass, sprinkle green glitter on infield.

4. Tint ½ cup frosting red; pipe lettering on corners of cake. Position cars and checkered flags.

NOTE *Edible glitter is available from Wilton Industries. Call 800-794-5866 or visit wilton.com.*

BUTTERCREAM BLAST LAYER CAKE

The decorations on this patriotic dessert remind me of a fireworks display.
Since the recipe includes both cookies and cake, people can take their pick or have both!
—JENNIFER LINDSTROM BROOKFIELD, WI

PREP: 1 HOUR 20 MIN. • **BAKE:** 25 MIN. + COOLING • **MAKES:** 12 SERVINGS

- 1 **package white cake mix (regular size)**
- 1 **tube (16½ ounces) refrigerated sugar cookie dough, softened**
- ⅔ **cup all-purpose flour**
- 12 **lollipop sticks**

BUTTERCREAM
- 1¼ **cups shortening**
- ⅓ **cup plus 4 teaspoons water**
- 1¼ **teaspoons vanilla extract**
- 5 **cups confectioners' sugar**
- 1 **tablespoon plus ¾ teaspoon meringue powder**

DECORATING
- **Red and blue colored sugar**
- **Coarse sugar**
- **Red and blue paste food coloring**
- 1 **tablespoon light corn syrup**

1. Prepare and bake the cake according to package directions, using two greased 9-in. round baking pans. Cool for 10 minutes before removing from pans to wire racks to cool completely.

2. In a large bowl, combine cookie dough and flour. On a lightly floured surface, roll out dough to ¼-in. thickness. Cut out 12 cookies with a floured 2-in. star cookie cutter; insert lollipop sticks into dough. Cut out eight cookies with a floured 1-in. star cookie cutter. Place 1 in. apart on ungreased baking sheets.

3. Bake at 350° for 7-9 minutes or until edges are light golden brown. Cool on wire racks.

4. For buttercream, using a heavy-duty stand mixer, combine the shortening, water and vanilla. Combine confectioners' sugar and meringue powder; beat into shortening mixture.

5. Spread 2 cups buttercream between layers and over top and sides of cake. Sprinkle the top with colored sugar. Frost cookie pops; sprinkle with red, blue and clear sugars. Tint ⅓ cup frosting red and ⅓ cup blue; leave the remaining frosting white. Using a #18 star tip and white frosting, pipe a border around bottom of cake. Using a #4 round tip with blue frosting and an additional #18 star tip with red frosting, pipe four flags on sides of cake.

6. In a microwave, heat corn syrup for 10 seconds or just until bubbly. Brush over one side of small star cookies; sprinkle with red and blue sugars. Press onto sides of cake. Press cookie pops into top of cake.

NOTE *Meringue powder is available from Wilton Industries. Call 800-794-5866 or visit wilton.com.*

FLOWERS AND VINES CAKE

This any-occasion cake may look sophisticated, but it's a cinch to prepare.
Be creative with your flower designs and colors.
—TASTE OF HOME TEST KITCHEN

PREP: 30 MIN. • **BAKE:** 25 MIN. + COOLING • **MAKES:** 12 SERVINGS

1 **package white cake mix (regular size)**
1 **can (16 ounces) vanilla frosting**
  Red licorice twists
  Red shoestring licorice
  Jelly beans
  Nonpareils

1. Prepare and bake cake mix according to package directions, using two greased 9-in. round baking pans. Cool for 10 minutes before removing from pans to wire racks to cool completely.

2. Spread frosting between layers and over top and sides of cake. Lightly press licorice twists around bottom edge of cake. Lightly press licorice and candies into cake forming flower and vine designs.

BASKETBALL CAKE

This fun cake is a slam-dunk to make because no special pan is needed. It scored big points at a dinner held for the church basketball team my husband coached.
—LONNA LICCINI CLIFTON, VA

PREP: 20 MIN. • **BAKE:** 1 HOUR + COOLING • **MAKES:** 12-16 SERVINGS

1 **package chocolate cake mix (regular size)**
1½ **cups canned vanilla frosting**
  Orange paste food coloring
4 **pieces black shoestring licorice**

1. Prepare cake batter according to package directions. Pour into a greased and floured 2½-qt. ovenproof bowl.

2. Bake at 350° for 60-70 minutes or until a toothpick inserted near the center comes out clean. Cool for 10 minutes before removing from the bowl to a wire rack to cool completely.

3. In a small bowl, combine frosting and food coloring. Place cake on a serving plate. Spread with frosting. Gently press a meat mallet into frosting so texture resembles a basketball. For the seams, gently press licorice into frosting.

PURSE CAKE

What a stylish idea! Celebrate a teenage girl's birthday or top off a day of Christmas shopping with this purse-shaped cake. It's easy to create—no special baking pan required.

—MICHELLE MENJOULET MURPHY, TX

PREP: 1½ HOURS • **BAKE:** 30 MIN. + COOLING • **MAKES:** 9 SERVINGS

- 1 **package white cake mix (regular size)**
- 2 **eggs**
- 1⅓ **cups water**

FROSTING

- ¾ **cup shortening**
- ¾ **cup butter, softened**
- 6 **cups confectioners' sugar**
- ¼ **cup milk**
- 1½ **teaspoons clear vanilla extract**
  Paste food coloring of your choice
  Silver dragees
- 1 **piece wired ribbon (10-inches)**
- 1 **plastic drinking straw, cut into 3-in. pieces**

1. In a large bowl, combine the cake mix, eggs and water; beat on low speed for 30 seconds. Beat on medium for 2 minutes. Pour 4 cups batter into a greased and waxed paper-lined 9-in. square baking pan (discard remaining batter).

2. Bake at 350° for 30-35 minutes or until a toothpick inserted near the center comes out clean. Cool for 10 minutes before removing from the pan to a wire rack to cool completely.

3. For frosting, in a large bowl, beat shortening and butter until light and fluffy. Add confectioners' sugar, milk and vanilla; beat until smooth. Tint frosting as desired.

4. Using a serrated knife, level top of cake if necessary. Using dental floss, cut cake in half diagonally by starting at a top edge and pulling floss through to opposite bottom edge. Place the cakes together with wide ends at bottom, forming a triangle. Cut off top 3 in.; spread frosting between layers.

5. Transfer cake to a serving platter; spread frosting over the top and sides of cake. Decorate as desired with remaining frosting and dragees. For handle, insert each end of ribbon into a drinking straw; insert each end into top of cake. Store in the refrigerator.

FLYING BAT CAKE

Packaged cake mix and cookies speed along the preparation of this spooky cake.
It can make an easy and impressive centerpiece on your Halloween treat table.

—TASTE OF HOME TEST KITCHEN

PREP: 20 MIN. • **BAKE:** 35 MIN. + COOLING • **MAKES:** 10 SERVINGS

1 **package carrot cake mix (regular size)**
5 **soft chocolate fudge cookies (about 3 inches)**
1 **can (16 ounces) buttercream frosting**
1 **tube blue decorating gel**

1. Prepare cake batter according to package directions. Pour into a greased 10-in. springform pan; place on a baking sheet. Bake at 350° for 35-40 minutes or until a toothpick inserted near the center comes out clean. Cool for 10 minutes before removing sides of pan; invert onto a wire rack. Cool completely.

2. With a 2-in. bat-shaped cookie cutter, cut out five bats from cookies. Place cookie trimmings in a food processor. Cover and pulse until coarse crumbs form; set aside.

3. Set aside 1 tablespoon frosting. Frost top and sides of cake with remaining frosting; press the reserved crumbs into sides. For moon, press a 4-in. round cookie cutter into frosting. Pipe blue gel over cake top for sky. With a narrow spatula, carefully spread gel over cake. Remove cookie cutter. Arrange bats on top. Using reserved frosting, pipe eyes on each bat.

BLACK FOREST CAKE

When my daughter went to Germany on a backpacking trip, she said the streets were lined with pastry shops.
Here's an easy take on one of the country's most popular desserts.

—PATRICIA RUTHERFORD WINCHESTER, IL

PREP: 10 MIN. • **BAKE:** 25 MIN. + CHILLING • **MAKES:** 6-8 SERVINGS

1 package (9 ounces) devil's food cake mix
½ cup water
1 egg
1 package (3 ounces) cream cheese, softened
2 tablespoons sugar
1 carton (8 ounces) frozen whipped topping, thawed
1 can (21 ounces) cherry pie filling

1. In a small bowl, beat the cake mix, water and egg on medium speed for 3-4 minutes. Pour into a greased 9-in. springform pan; place pan on a baking sheet.
2. Bake at 350° for 23-25 minutes or until cake springs back when lightly touched. Cool completely on a wire rack.
3. In a small bowl, beat cream cheese and sugar until fluffy; fold in whipped topping. Spread the pie filling over cake; top with the cream cheese mixture. Cover and refrigerate for 4 hours. Remove sides of the pan. Store in the refrigerator.

CAKE WITH BUTTERCREAM DECORATING FROSTING

The lovely design in the frosting is an impressive way to dress up your favorite cake mix.
It does take some time, but it is surprisingly easy to do!

—TASTE OF HOME TEST KITCHEN

PREP: 1 HOUR • **BAKE:** 25 MIN. + COOLING • **MAKES:** 12 SERVINGS

- 1 **package cake mix of your choice (regular size)**
- ¾ **cup butter, softened**
- ¾ **cup shortening**
- 2 **teaspoons vanilla extract**
- ⅛ **teaspoon salt**
- 9 **cups confectioners' sugar**
- ½ **to ¾ cup whole milk**
  Pink paste food coloring or color of your choice

1. Prepare and bake cake mix according to package directions, using two 9-in. round baking pans.

2. In a large bowl, beat butter, shortening, vanilla and salt until blended. Beat in confectioners' sugar alternately with milk, adding enough milk to reach desired consistency; beat until frosting is smooth.

3. Place one cake layer on a serving plate; spread with 1 cup frosting. Top with remaining cake layer. Spread a thin layer of the frosting over top and sides of cake, using no more than 1 cup of the frosting.

4. Remove 1 cup frosting to each of two small bowls; tint 1 cup frosting light pink and leave 1 cup frosting white. Tint remaining frosting dark pink.

5. Cut a small hole in the tip of three pastry bags or in a corner of three food-safe plastic bags; insert the same-size medium round tip in each. Fill each with a different color frosting.

6. To decorate side of cake, pipe a row of four evenly spaced ½-in. dots down side of cake, making one white dot, one light pink dot and two dark pink dots. Using the back of teaspoons from your flatware (a different one for each color), gently swipe each dot to the right. Repeat with additional rows, piping each new row of dots to the right of the previous row,

until side of the cake is almost completely covered. Pipe a final row of dots to fill the uncovered section of cake side.

7. To decorate top of cake, make concentric circles of different colored frosting, piping dots one at a time and swiping each dot before piping another. In center, pipe four dots of same color; swipe each dot toward the center.

EASTER BASKET CAKE

For a festive cake all of your guests will be impressed with at your Easter gathering,
try this. It's deceptively easy! Enjoy stocking the basket with your favorite springtime goodies.

—MARY KAY MORRIS COKATO, MN

PREP: 1 HOUR • **BAKE:** 30 MIN. • **MAKES:** 10-12 SERVINGS

- 1 **package yellow cake mix (regular size)**
- 3 **cups of white frosting**
- 3 **drops of green food coloring**
- ½ **teaspoon of water**
- 2 **cups of flaked coconut
  Jelly beans, marshmallow
  Peeps and chocolate kisses
  (or the candy of your
  choice)**

1. Cover a serving board with gift wrap, taping the wrap on the back side of the board. Cover wrapped board with clear cellophane in the same way. Set the board aside.

2. Using two 9-in. round baking pans, prepare and bake the cake according to package directions. Cool cakes for 10 minutes before removing from the pans to wire racks to cool completely.

3. Place one cake in the center of the covered serving board. Spread the top of the cake with frosting.

4. Cut a 6-in. circle from the center of the second cake. Remove the center circle and set aside for another use. Place the cake ring on top of the frosted cake layer, creating the basket. Frost top and sides of basket.

5. For the handle, cover a 14-in. x ¾-in. strip of lightweight cardboard with plastic wrap. Bend the cardboard strip into an upside-down "U" shape and insert the ends into the top of the cake about 1 in. from the outside edge. Frost the handle.

6. In a large resealable plastic bag, combine three drops of the green food coloring and ½ teaspoon of water. Add the coconut; seal the bag and shake until coconut is evenly tinted. Sprinkle a portion of the green coconut inside the basket. Reserve remaining coconut to sprinkle around the bottom of basket later.

7. Fill the basket with candy of your choice. Press candy pieces onto the top of the handle where shown in the photo or as desired.

8. When the frosting on the cake is firm, press the tines of a fork into the frosting on the sides of the cake to create a basket-weave pattern, alternating vertical and horizontal designs.

9. Sprinkle the remaining tinted coconut around the bottom of the basket.

ROCKY ROAD CAKE

This creative take on classic rocky road flavors creates a showstopping and absolutely delectable dessert.
—TASTE OF HOME TEST KITCHEN

PREP: 30 MIN. • **BAKE:** 25 MIN. + COOLING • **MAKES:** 12 SERVINGS

1 **package chocolate cake mix (regular size)**
1 **can (16 ounces) chocolate frosting**
1¾ **cups dry roasted peanuts, divided**
1½ **cups miniature milk chocolate kisses**
1½ **cups miniature marshmallows, divided**

1. Prepare and bake the cake according to package directions, using two greased 9-in. round baking pans. Cool for 10 minutes before removing from pans to wire racks to cool completely.

2. Spread frosting between layers and over top and sides of cake. In a large bowl, combine 1½ cups peanuts, the chocolate kisses and 1 cup marshmallows; set aside.

3. Arrange the remaining marshmallows to form the border of a road across the top of cake. Coarsely chop remaining peanuts and sprinkle inside marshmallow border. Lightly press remaining chocolate mixture over sides and top of cake.

RED VELVET HEART TORTE

I bake this scrumptious, fruit-topped layer cake every February 14 for my husband's birthday. The heart shape is really pretty for Valentine's Day.
—AMY FREITAG STANFORD, IL

PREP: 25 MIN. • **BAKE:** 30 MIN. + COOLING • **MAKES:** 14 SERVINGS

- 1 package red velvet cake mix (regular size)
- 1 carton (6 ounces) raspberry yogurt
- ⅓ cup confectioners' sugar
- 1 carton (12 ounces) frozen whipped topping, thawed
- 1 cup raspberry pie filling

1. Prepare cake batter according to package directions. Pour into two greased and floured 9-in. heart-shaped baking pans.

2. Bake at 350° for 30-33 minutes or until a toothpick inserted near the center comes out clean. Cool for 10 minutes before removing from the pans to wire racks to cool completely.

3. In a large bowl, combine yogurt and confectioners' sugar; fold in whipped topping. Cut each cake horizontally into two layers. Place bottom layer on a serving plate; top with a fourth of the yogurt mixture. Repeat the layers three times. Spread the pie filling over the top to within 1 in. of edges. Store in the refrigerator.

OCEAN CAKE

Whether it's for a pool or birthday party, this fish-themed cake will snag smiles from kids of all ages!
—TASTE OF HOME TEST KITCHEN

PREP: 30 MIN. • **BAKE:** 25 MIN. + COOLING • **MAKES:** 12 SERVINGS

- 1 package white cake mix (regular size)
- 2⅔ cups canned vanilla frosting
  Blue and green Fruit Roll-Ups
  Fish candies
  Black shoestring licorice
  Candy stick

1. Prepare and bake the cake according to package directions, using two greased 9-in. round baking pans. Cool for 10 minutes before removing from pans to wire racks to cool completely.

2. Spread 1⅔ cups frosting between layers and over top and sides of cake. Using the back of a spoon, make waves on the top of cake with remaining frosting.

3. Cut wave shapes out of the fruit roll-ups; gently press along bottom of cake. Arrange additional wave shapes and fish candies on top of cake as desired. Tie licorice on one end of candy stick to create a fishing pole.

HOW-TO *To create ocean waves, smooth frosting first. Then use the back of a spoon to make a small twisting motion in one direction. Next, move spoon over slightly and make another twist the opposite way. Repeat. Cut the fruit roll-ups in half vertically. Then fold in half, keeping the plastic sides together. Cut into wave shapes.*

CANDY LAND CAKE

My friend asked me to make her son's 5th birthday cake. I asked her what he wanted on it and she said, Oh, just put on gobs and gobs of candy! Instead of haphazardly piling on the sweets, I made it like the Candy Land board game. The birthday boy, his friends and family members loved it!

—PEN PEREZ BERKELEY, CA

PREP: 2 HOURS • **BAKE:** 30 MIN. + COOLING • **MAKES:** 30-40 SERVINGS

2 **packages cake mix of your choice (regular size)**
Vanilla and chocolate frosting
Green mist food color spray, optional
Assorted decorations: Starburst candies, red Fruit Roll-Up, red coarse sugar, Dots, regular and miniature peanut butter cups, chocolate jimmies, large and small gumdrops, Dum Dum pops, miniature candy canes, clear and blue rock candy, cake and waffle ice cream cones, multicolored sprinkles, green colored sugar, miniature marshmallows, round peppermints and conversation hearts

1. Line two 13x9-in. baking pans with waxed paper and grease the paper. Prepare cake batter; pour into the prepared pans. Bake according to package directions. Cool 15 minutes before removing from pans to wire racks to cool completely; remove waxed paper.
2. Level tops of cakes; place side by side on a covered board. Frost top and sides of cake with vanilla frosting; mist with food color spray if desired.
3. With Candy Land game board as your guide, form a path using Starburst candies. With vanilla frosting, pipe "Happy Birthday" on candies. With chocolate frosting, make an arrow; pipe "Start" on the arrow with vanilla frosting.
4. For the Mountain/Gumdrop pass, use a red Fruit Roll-Up, red coarse sugar and Dots.
5. For forests, add peanut butter cups topped with piped chocolate frosting, chocolate jimmies, gumdrops, Dum Dum pops, candy canes and rock candy.
6. For castle, pipe vanilla frosting onto ice cream cones. Garnish with Dots and sprinkles.
7. Between the pathways, add green colored sugar, sprinkles, miniature marshmallows, peppermints and conversation hearts. Pipe additional frosting to fill in spaces; top with sprinkles.
8. Pipe vanilla frosting around base of cake; place peppermints around top edge of cake.
NOTE *This cake is best eaten the day it's prepared. Do not refrigerate.*

BROWN BEAR CAKE

Ideal for a young child's birthday, the bear cake is sure to bring smiles to the guest of honor.

—TASTE OF HOME TEST KITCHEN

PREP: 1½ HOURS • **BAKE:** 40 MIN. + COOLING • **MAKES:** 18-20 SERVINGS

- **2 packages chocolate cake mix (regular size)**
- **4 ounces cream cheese, softened**
- **1 tablespoon butter, softened**
- **4 cups confectioners' sugar**
- **⅓ cup baking cocoa**
- **¼ cup milk**
- **3 cups flaked coconut, divided Brown gel food coloring**
- **5 chocolate-covered peppermint patties**
- **16 brown milk chocolate M&M's**
- **2 dark chocolate kisses**
- **5 pieces red shoestring licorice**

1. Prepare cake mixes according to package directions. Pour 3 cups batter into a greased and floured 2-qt. round baking dish. Pour 1½ cups batter into a greased and floured 1-qt. ovenproof bowl. Using remaining batter, fill six greased jumbo muffin cups and four greased regular muffin cups two-thirds full.

2. Bake cupcakes for 18-20 minutes and cakes for 40-45 minutes at 350° or until a toothpick inserted near the center comes out clean. Cool cupcakes and cakes for 10 minutes before removing from the pans to wire racks to cool completely.

3. Level the top of the cakes, four jumbo cupcakes and two regular cupcakes. (Save the remaining cupcakes for another use.) Place large cake top side down on an 18-in. x 12-in. covered board. For teddy bear's head, place the small cake top side down above large cake. Position jumbo cupcakes cut side up for arms and legs. Place regular cupcakes on top of head for ears.

4. In a large bowl, beat the cream cheese and butter until smooth. Add the confectioners' sugar, cocoa and milk; beat until smooth. Frost tops and sides of cakes and cupcakes. Tint 2¼ cups coconut dark brown; tint remaining coconut light brown.

5. Sprinkle dark brown coconut over arms and legs. Leaving a 4-in. circle in center of bear's body, sprinkle dark brown coconut in a 1-inch circle around edge of cake. Sprinkle dark brown coconut in a ½-in. circle around edges of the head and ears. Press dark brown coconut into the sides of the body, head and ears. Sprinkle light brown coconut over the middle of the body, head and ears.

6. Position one peppermint patty on face for nose. Place one peppermint patty and four M&M's on each paw. Insert chocolate kisses point side down for eyes. Cut one licorice piece into two 2-in. strips; shape to form a mouth. Cut two licorice pieces into a 7-in. strip; place around the neck. Shape the remaining licorice into a bow; place below neck. Store in the refrigerator.

POLKA DOT CAKE

With a few simple ingredients, you can create this fun cake for a kid's or even adult's polka-dotty party. Change the color scheme by using different flavored Fruit Roll-Ups.

—**FLO BURTNETT** GAGE, OK

PREP: 20 MIN. • **BAKE:** 20 MIN.
MAKES: 12 SERVINGS

- 1 **package chocolate cake mix (regular size)**
- 1 **can (16 ounces) vanilla frosting**
- 1 **package (5 ounces) Fruit Roll-Ups**
  Round cookie cutters: 1 inch, 1½ inches, 2 inches and 2¾ inches

1. Prepare and bake the cake according to package directions, using two greased and floured 9-in. round baking pans. Cool for 10 minutes before removing from the pans to wire racks to cool completely.

2. Spread frosting between layers and over top and sides of cake. Unroll Fruit Roll-Ups. Using the cookie cutters and a variety of Fruit Roll-Up colors, cut out circles. Arrange circles on top and sides of cake.

FLAG CAKE

Get ready to hear oohs and aahs! This stars-and-stripes cake is sure to light up your Fourth of July party or other patriotic celebration.

—TASTE OF HOME TEST KITCHEN

PREP: 1½ HOURS + CHILLING • **BAKE:** 35 MIN. + COOLING • **MAKES:** 15 SERVINGS

- **1 package French vanilla cake mix (regular size)**
- **1 cup buttermilk**
- **⅓ cup canola oil**
- **4 eggs**

FILLING
- **1 package (3 ounces) berry blue gelatin**
- **1½ cups boiling water, divided**
- **1 cup cold water, divided**
- **Ice cubes**
- **1 package (3 ounces) strawberry gelatin**
- **⅔ cup finely chopped fresh strawberries**
- **¼ cup fresh blueberries**

FROSTING
- **¾ cup butter, softened**
- **2 cups confectioners' sugar**
- **1 tablespoon 2% milk**
- **1 jar (7 ounces) marshmallow creme**

1. Line a 13-in. x 9-in. baking pan with waxed paper and grease the paper; set aside. In a large bowl, combine first four ingredients; beat on low speed for 30 seconds. Beat on medium for 2 minutes. Pour into prepared pan.

2. Bake at 350° for 35-40 minutes or until a toothpick inserted near the center comes out clean. Cool for 10 minutes before removing from the pan to a wire rack to cool completely.

3. Transfer cake to a covered cake board. Using a small knife, cut out a 5-in. x 4-in. rectangle (½ inch deep) in the top left corner of cake, leaving a ½-in. border along edges of cake. For red stripes, cut out ½-in.-wide rows (½ in. deep), leaving a ½-in. border. Using a fork, carefully remove cut-out cake pieces.

4. In a small bowl, dissolve berry blue gelatin in ¾ cup boiling water. Pour ½ cup cold water into a 2-cup measuring cup; add enough ice cubes to measure 1¼ cups. Stir into the gelatin until slightly thickened. Scoop out and discard any remaining ice cubes. Repeat, making the strawberry gelatin.

5. In a small bowl, combine the strawberries and 1 cup strawberry gelatin. In another bowl, combine blueberries and 1 cup blue gelatin. Refrigerate for 20 minutes or just until soft-set. (Save the remaining gelatin for another use.)

6. Stir gelatin mixtures. Slowly pour blueberry mixture into rectangle; spoon strawberry mixture into stripes.

7. In a large bowl, beat butter until fluffy; beat in confectioners' sugar and milk until smooth. Add marshmallow creme; beat well until light and fluffy. Spread 1 cup over sides and top edge of cake. Refrigerate remaining frosting for 20 minutes.

8. Cut a small hole in the corner of pastry or plastic bag; insert a large star tip. Fill the bag with remaining frosting. Pipe frosting in between rows of strawberry gelatin and around edges of cake. Refrigerate for 1-2 hours or until gelatin is set. Store in the refrigerator.

CONGRATULATIONS SENIORS CAKE

I decorated a special cake for my son's high school graduation.
Each of the frosted figures had hair color and details to resemble his friends.

—SHERRI FROHLICH BENTON, AR

PREP: 1 HOUR • **BAKE:** 45 MIN. + COOLING • **MAKES:** 15-20 SERVINGS

1 **package yellow cake mix
   (regular size)**
4 **cups vanilla frosting
   Paste food coloring in
   colors of your choice**

1. Prepare and bake the cake according to the package directions, using a greased 13-in. x 9-in. baking pan. Cool for 10 minutes before removing from the pan to a wire rack to cool completely.

2. Level top of cake; place on a serving platter. Tint frosting desired colors; spread over top and sides of cake. Pipe a shell border, caps, gowns and desired message.

CIRCUS CAKE

Ideal for a child's party, this whimsical cake steals the show with its cotton candy topping and cookie-laced sides.

—TASTE OF HOME TEST KITCHEN

PREP: 30 MIN. • **BAKE:** 25 MIN. + COOLING • **MAKES:** 12 SERVINGS

1 **package white cake mix
   (regular size)**
1 **can (16 ounces) vanilla
   frosting
   Nerds candies
   Miniature chocolate cream-
   filled chocolate sandwich
   cookies
   Frosted animal crackers
   Miniature marshmallows**

   **Cotton candy
   Lollipops**

1. Prepare and bake the cake according to package directions, using two greased 9-in. round baking pans. Cool for 10 minutes before removing from pans to wire racks to cool completely.

2. Spread frosting between layers and over top and sides of cake. Lightly press the Nerds, sandwich cookies and animal crackers onto sides of cake. Arrange the marshmallows along edge of cake. Just before serving, arrange the cotton candy and lollipops on top of cake.

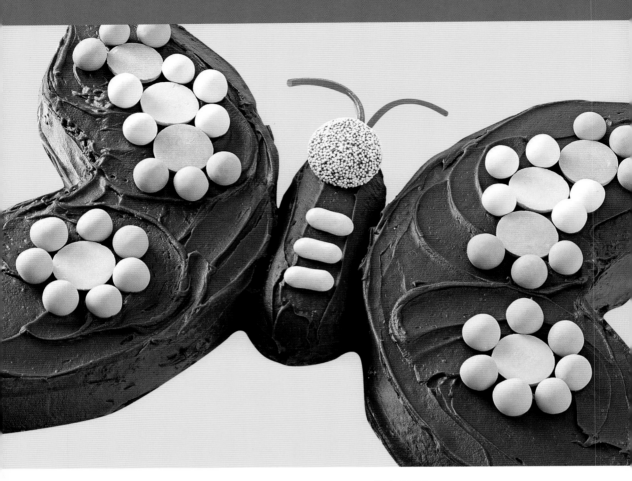

BUTTERFLY CAKE

The colorful cake we created will set taste buds aflutter and give your next warm-weather gathering a bright lift!

—TASTE OF HOME TEST KITCHEN

PREP: 30 MIN. • **BAKE:** 25 MIN. + STANDING • **MAKES:** 8 SERVINGS

- **1 package yellow cake mix (regular size)**
- **1 individual cream-filled sponge cake**
- **1 can (16 ounces) chocolate frosting**
  Red shoestring licorice
  Assorted candies of your choice

1. Prepare cake batter according to package directions, using two greased and floured 9-in. round baking pans.

2. Bake at 350° for 25-30 minutes or until a toothpick inserted near the center comes out clean. Cool for 10 minutes before removing from the pans to wire racks to cool completely.

3. Cut one cake in half widthwise. (Save the second cake for another use.) Cut a notch from the center of each cut side to define outer edges of wings. Cut corners of wings so they are slightly rounded. Let cake stand for 2 hours.

4. On a serving platter, position the cake halves on each side of sponge cake. Frost top and sides of butterfly with chocolate frosting. Cut licorice into two small pieces; push ends into top of sponge cake for antennae. Decorate with candies.

Crowd Pleasers

102

Chocolate Peanut Butter Cake

110

Raspberry Cake

114

Coconut Poppy Seed Cake

CHOCOLATE PEANUT BUTTER CAKE

The two great flavors of chocolate and peanut butter come together in this oh-so-easy and delicious cake. Kids of every age will be all over this one!

—BRENDA MELANCON MCCOMB, MS

PREP: 10 MIN. • **BAKE:** 30 MIN. + COOLING • **MAKES:** 12-15 SERVINGS

  2 cups miniature marshmallows
  1 package chocolate cake mix (regular size)
1¼ cups water
  ¾ cup peanut butter
  ⅓ cup canola oil
  3 eggs
  1 cup (6 ounces) semisweet chocolate chips

1. Sprinkle marshmallows into a greased 13x9-in. baking pan. In a large bowl, combine the cake mix, water, peanut butter, oil and eggs; beat on low speed for 30 seconds. Beat on medium for 2 minutes or until smooth. Pour over the marshmallows; sprinkle with the chocolate chips.

2. Bake at 350° for 30-35 minutes or until a toothpick inserted near the center comes out clean. Cool on a wire rack.

TASTES LIKE EGGNOG CAKE

My holiday eggnog cake comes out perfect every time. It always gets compliments, and most people think that I spend hours in the kitchen working on it! My husband's colleagues at work ask for it every Christmas.

—LISA BARRETT DURANGO, CO

PREP: 30 MIN. • **BAKE:** 25 MIN. + COOLING • **MAKES:** 12-15 SERVINGS

  1 package yellow cake mix (regular size)
  1 teaspoon ground nutmeg
  ¼ teaspoon ground ginger
FROSTING
1½ cups heavy whipping cream
  3 tablespoons confectioners' sugar
  1 teaspoon rum extract

1. Prepare cake batter according to the package directions, adding nutmeg and ginger to the dry ingredients. Pour into a greased 13x9-in. baking pan.

2. Bake at 350° for 25-30 minutes or until a toothpick inserted near the center comes out clean. Cool on a wire rack.

3. For frosting, in a small bowl, beat cream and confectioners' sugar until stiff peaks form. Fold in extract. Spread over cake. Store in the refrigerator.

PINEAPPLE PUDDING CAKE

My mother used to love making this easy dessert in the summertime.
It's refreshing and wonderful—like a perfect summer day!

—KATHLEEN WORDEN NORTH ANDOVER, MA

PREP: 25 MIN. • **BAKE:** 15 MIN. + CHILLING • **MAKES:** 20 SERVINGS

- 1 package (9 ounces) yellow cake mix
- 1½ cups cold fat-free milk
- 1 package (1 ounce) sugar-free instant vanilla pudding mix
- 1 package (8 ounces) fat-free cream cheese
- 1 can (20 ounces) unsweetened crushed pineapple, well drained
- 1 carton (8 ounces) frozen fat-free whipped topping, thawed
- ¼ cup chopped walnuts, toasted
- 20 maraschino cherries, well drained

1. Prepare the cake mix batter according to package directions; pour into a 13x9-in. baking pan coated with cooking spray.

2. Bake at 350° for 15-20 minutes or until a toothpick inserted near the center comes out clean. Cool completely on a wire rack.

3. In a large bowl, whisk the milk and pudding mix for 2 minutes. Let stand for 2 minutes or until soft-set.

4. In a small bowl, beat cream cheese until smooth. Beat in pudding mixture until blended. Spread evenly over cake. Sprinkle with pineapple; spread with the whipped topping. Sprinkle with the walnuts and garnish with the cherries. Store in the refrigerator.

CREAM-FILLED CHOCOLATE CAKE

This simple sweet will go fast at any potluck. It gets a homemade taste
from a yummy vanilla layer and from-scratch frosting.
—LINDA HARTSELL APPLE CREEK, OH

PREP: 35 MIN. + FREEZING • **BAKE:** 20 MIN. + COOLING • **MAKES:** 16-20 SERVINGS

1 **package chocolate cake mix
  (regular size)**
5 **tablespoons all-purpose flour**
1¼ **cups milk**
½ **cup butter, softened**
½ **cup shortening**
1 **cup sugar**
  Pinch salt
FROSTING
½ **cup butter, softened**
¼ **cup baking cocoa**
1 **teaspoon vanilla extract**
3 **cups confectioners' sugar**
4 **to 5 tablespoons hot water**

1. Prepare cake batter according
to package directions; pour into a
greased 15x10x1-in. baking pan.
Bake at 350° for 20-25 minutes or
until a toothpick inserted near
the center comes out clean. Cool
on a wire rack.

2. Meanwhile, for filling, mix
the flour and milk in a saucepan
until smooth. Bring to a boil over
medium heat, stirring frequently.
Cook and stir for 2 minutes;
remove from the heat and cool
completely.

3. In a bowl, cream the butter,
shortening, sugar and salt until
fluffy. Add flour mixture; beat
until fluffy, about 4 minutes.
Spread over cake. Freeze for
15 minutes.

4. For frosting, beat butter, cocoa
and vanilla in a bowl until fluffy.
Beat in confectioners' sugar and
water. Spread over the filling.
Store in the refrigerator.

FAST FIX # CHOCOLATE UPSIDE-DOWN CAKE

Here's a dessert that's simply out of this world. All of your guests will agree that it's the best ever.
Enjoy it with a scoop of vanilla ice cream.

—**IOLA EGLE** BELLA VISTA, AR

PREP: 15 MIN. • **BAKE:** 55 MIN. + COOLING • **MAKES:** 12-15 SERVINGS

1¼ cups water
¼ cup butter, cubed
1 cup packed brown sugar
1 cup flaked coconut
2 cups (12 ounces) semisweet chocolate chips
1 cup chopped pecans
2 cups miniature marshmallows
1 package German chocolate cake mix (regular size)

1. Preheat oven to 325°. In a small saucepan, heat water and butter until butter is melted. Stir in brown sugar; mix well. Pour into a greased 13x9-in. baking pan. Sprinkle with coconut, chocolate chips, pecans and marshmallows.

2. Prepare cake batter according to package directions; carefully pour over marshmallows. Bake cake 55-60 minutes or until a toothpick inserted in center comes out clean. Cool 10 minutes before inverting cake onto a serving plate.

PINEAPPLE ORANGE CAKE

This is one of my favorite cakes...it's so satisfying. I've been adapting it for years and now it's almost guilt-free.

—**PAM SJOLUND** COLUMBIA, SC

PREP: 15 MIN.
BAKE: 25 MIN. + CHILLING
MAKES: 15 SERVINGS

- 1 **package yellow cake mix (regular size)**
- 1 **can (11 ounces) mandarin oranges, undrained**
- 4 **egg whites**
- ½ **cup unsweetened applesauce**

TOPPING

- 1 **can (20 ounces) crushed pineapple, undrained**
- 1 **package (1 ounce) sugar-free instant vanilla pudding mix**
- 1 **carton (8 ounces) reduced-fat whipped topping**

1. In a large bowl, beat the cake mix, oranges, egg whites and applesauce on low speed for 2 minutes. Pour into a 13x9-in. baking dish coated with cooking spray.

2. Bake at 350° for 25-30 minutes or until a toothpick inserted near the center comes out clean. Cool on a wire rack.

3. In a bowl, combine pineapple and pudding mix. Fold in the whipped topping just until blended. Spread over the cake. Refrigerate for at least 1 hour before serving. Store in the refrigerator.

BOSTON CREAM PIE

My impressive dessert can be made without much fuss. It's pretty, tasty and always popular at picnics and potlucks.

—CLARA HONEYAGER NORTH PRAIRIE, WI

PREP: 45 MIN. + CHILLING • **BAKE:** 1 HOUR • **MAKES:** 96 SERVINGS

- **4 packages yellow cake mix (regular size)**
- **11 cups cold milk**
- **4 packages (5.1 ounces each) instant vanilla pudding mix**
- **4 jars (16 ounces each) hot fudge ice cream topping, warmed**
- **96 maraschino cherries with stems, optional**

1. Prepare and bake the cakes according to package directions, using four greased 13x9-in. baking pans. Cool completely on wire racks.

2. Meanwhile, in a large bowl, beat milk and pudding mixes on low for 2-3 minutes. Cover; chill for at least 30 minutes. Cut each cake into 24 pieces; split each piece horizontally. Place about 1 heaping tablespoon of pudding between layers. Spread each with 1 tablespoon fudge topping and garnish with a cherry if desired. Store in the refrigerator.

FAST FIX > SWEET POTATO CRANBERRY CAKE

This recipe uses delicious items you have in your pantry, like sweet potatoes, cranberries, coconut and chocolate chips. The secret ingredient, however, is a bit of chili powder.

—AMIE VALPONE NEW YORK, NY

PREP: 15 MIN. • **BAKE:** 30 MIN. + COOLING • **MAKES:** 20 SERVINGS

- **1 package white cake mix (regular size)**
- **2 cups mashed sweet potatoes**
- **½ cup buttermilk**
- **2 eggs**
- **2 tablespoons canola oil**
- **1 teaspoon vanilla extract**
- **1 package (8 ounces) reduced-fat cream cheese**
- **¾ cup confectioners' sugar**
- **1 teaspoon ground cinnamon**
- **¾ teaspoon chili powder**

- **½ cup dried cranberries**
- **⅓ cup flaked coconut, toasted**
- **¼ cup dark chocolate chips**

1. In a large bowl, combine cake mix, sweet potatoes, buttermilk, eggs, oil and vanilla; beat on low speed for 30 seconds. Beat on medium for 2 minutes.

2. Pour into a 13x9-in. baking pan coated with cooking spray. Bake at 350° for 28-33 minutes or until

a toothpick inserted near the center comes out clean. Cool on a wire rack.

3. In a small bowl, combine the cream cheese, confectioners' sugar, cinnamon and chili powder. Spread over the cake. Sprinkle with the cranberries, coconut and chocolate chips. Store in the refrigerator.

RASPBERRY CAKE

I jazz up a plain cake with raspberry gelatin and frozen berries. Spread with a light, fruity whipped topping, the festive results make a pleasant dessert.

—MARION ANDERSON DALTON, MN

PREP: 10 MIN. + CHILLING • **BAKE:** 35 MIN. + COOLING • **MAKES:** 12-16 SERVINGS

1 package white cake mix (regular size)
1 package (3 ounces) raspberry gelatin
4 eggs
½ cup canola oil
¼ cup hot water
1 package (10 ounces) frozen sweetened raspberries, thawed, undrained

FROSTING

1 carton (12 ounces) frozen whipped topping, thawed
1 package (10 ounces) frozen sweetened raspberries, thawed, undrained
Fresh raspberries, optional

1. In a large bowl, combine the cake mix, gelatin, eggs, oil and water; beat on low speed for 30 seconds. Beat on medium for 2 minutes. Stir in raspberries.
2. Pour into a greased 13x9-in. baking pan. Bake at 350° for 35-40 minutes or until a toothpick inserted near the center comes out clean. Cool.
3. For frosting, in a large bowl, fold whipped topping into raspberries. Spread over cake. Refrigerate for 2 hours before serving. Garnish with the fresh raspberries if desired. Store in the refrigerator.

LIGHTER PUMPKIN GOOEY BUTTER CAKE

With all of the original's decadence, this ooey-gooey dessert trims
64 calories and 5 grams fat, making it a guilt-free holiday treat!
—APRIL TAYLOR APO, AE

PREP: 20 MIN. • **BAKE:** 45 MIN. + COOLING • **MAKES:** 24 SERVINGS

1 **package yellow cake mix (regular size)**
1 **egg**
½ **cup reduced-fat butter, melted**

FILLING

1 **package (8 ounces) reduced-fat cream cheese**
1 **cup canned pumpkin**
½ **cup reduced-fat butter, melted**
2 **eggs, lightly beaten**
2 **egg whites**
1 **teaspoon vanilla extract**

2¾ **cups confectioners' sugar**
1 **teaspoon ground cinnamon**
1 **teaspoon ground nutmeg**
   Additional confectioners' sugar, optional

1. In a large bowl, beat the cake mix, egg and butter on low speed until combined. Press into a 13x9-in. baking pan coated with cooking spray.

2. In a another large bowl, beat cream cheese and pumpkin until smooth. Add the butter, eggs, egg whites and vanilla; beat on low until combined. Add the confectioners' sugar, cinnamon and nutmeg; mix well. Pour over the crust.

3. Bake at 350° for 45-50 minutes or until edges are golden brown. Cool completely on a wire rack. Chill until serving. Sprinkle with additional confectioners' sugar if desired. Store in the refrigerator.

FAST FIX CHOCOLATE CHIP SNACK CAKE

Every bite is chocolaty good in my sensational cake since is it loaded with chocolate chips and grated chocolate. I often make it for weekend guests and work luncheons.
—**KAREN WALKER** STERLING, VA

PREP: 15 MIN. • **BAKE:** 45 MIN. + COOLING • **MAKES:** 12-15 SERVINGS

1   **package yellow cake mix (regular size)**
1   **package (3.4 ounces) instant vanilla pudding mix**
4   **eggs**
1   **cup water**
½   **cup canola oil**
1   **package (12 ounces) miniature semisweet chocolate chips**
4   **ounces German sweet chocolate, grated, divided Confectioners' sugar**

1. In a large bowl, combine the first five ingredients; beat on low speed for 30 seconds. Beat on medium for 2 minutes. Stir in chocolate chips and half of the grated chocolate. Pour into a greased 13x9-in. baking pan.
2. Bake at 350° for 45-50 minutes or until a toothpick inserted near the center comes out clean.

3. Sprinkle with the remaining grated chocolate while slightly warm. Cool completely. Dust with confectioners' sugar.

FAST FIX SURPRISE SPICE CAKE

Canned tomato soup replaces some of the oil in this spice cake, decreasing the fat and brightening the cake's color.
—**HANNAH THOMPSON** SCOTTS VALLEY, CA

PREP: 15 MIN. • **BAKE:** 30 MIN. + COOLING • **MAKES:** 12 SERVINGS

1   **package spice cake mix (regular size)**
1   **can (10¾ ounces) condensed tomato soup, undiluted**
3   **eggs**
½   **cup water**
1   **can (16 ounces) cream cheese frosting**

1. In a large bowl, combine the cake mix, soup, eggs and water; beat on low speed for 30 seconds. Beat on medium for 2 minutes. Pour into a greased 13x9-in. baking dish.

2. Bake at 350° for 30-33 minutes or until a toothpick inserted near the center comes out clean. Cool on a wire rack. Frost with the cream cheese frosting. Store in the refrigerator.

FAST FIX COCONUT POPPY SEED CAKE

I'm known for my coconut cake and it is definitely one of my most-requested desserts. You can change it up by using different cake mixes and pudding flavors.

—GAIL CAYCE WAUTOMA, WI

PREP: 15 MIN.
BAKE: 20 MIN. + COOLING
MAKES: 20-24 SERVINGS

- 1 **package white cake mix (regular size)**
- ½ **cup flaked coconut**
- ¼ **cup poppy seeds**
- 3½ **cups cold milk**
- 1 **teaspoon coconut extract**
- 2 **packages (3.4 ounces each) instant vanilla pudding mix**
- 1 **carton (8 ounces) frozen whipped topping, thawed**
- ⅓ **cup flaked coconut, toasted, optional**

1. Prepare the cake according to package directions, adding the coconut and poppy seeds to batter. Pour into a greased 13x9-in. baking pan.

2. Bake at 350° for 20-25 minutes or until a toothpick inserted near the center comes out clean. Cool completely.

3. In a large bowl, whisk the milk, extract and pudding mixes for 2 minutes. Let stand for 2 minutes or until soft-set. Spread over the cake. Spread with the whipped topping. Sprinkle with toasted coconut if desired.

PINEAPPLE POKE CAKE

Here's a delicious dessert that's great every month of the year.
With several store-bought ingredients, it's a snap to prepare any time.

—SANDRA ETELAMAKI ISHPEMING, MI

PREP: 20 MIN. • **BAKE:** 25 MIN. + COOLING • **MAKES:** 20 SERVINGS

- 1 **package yellow cake mix (regular size)**
- 1 **package (1 ounce) sugar-free instant vanilla pudding mix**
- ½ **cup water**
- 2 **eggs, lightly beaten**
- ½ **cup egg substitute**
- ½ **cup fat-free milk**
- ¼ **cup unsweetened applesauce**
- 1 **can (8 ounces) unsweetened crushed pineapple, undrained**
- ¼ **cup packed brown sugar**

FROSTING

- 1½ **cups cold fat-free milk**
- 1 **package (1 ounce) sugar-free instant vanilla pudding mix**
- 1 **carton (8 ounces) frozen reduced-fat whipped topping, thawed**

1. In a large bowl, combine the first seven ingredients. Beat on medium speed for 2 minutes. Pour into a 13x9-in. baking pan coated with cooking spray.

2. Bake at 350° for 25-30 minutes or until a toothpick inserted near the center comes out clean.

3. Meanwhile, in a small saucepan, combine pineapple and brown sugar. Cook and stir until mixture comes to a boil. Boil for 4-5 minutes or until most of the liquid is evaporated; cool slightly. Remove cake from the oven; place on a wire rack. Poke holes in warm cake with a fork. Spoon pineapple mixture evenly over cake; cool completely.

4. For frosting, in a small bowl, whisk milk and pudding mix for 2 minutes. Let stand for 2 minutes or until soft-set. Spread over cake. Spread whipped topping over pudding. Store in the refrigerator.

MINT CHOCOLATE CAKE

My husband works for a mint farmer, so I'm always looking for recipes with mint in them. I received this recipe at my bridal shower. My friend wrote easy and pretty on the top corner of the recipe card—and it's so true.

—VIRGINIA HORST MESA, WA

PREP: 15 MIN. + CHILLING • **BAKE:** 25 MIN. + COOLING • **MAKES:** 20-24 SERVINGS

1 **package chocolate cake mix (regular size)**

FROSTING
- ½ **cup butter, softened**
- 2 **cups confectioners' sugar**
- 1 **tablespoon water**
- ½ **teaspoon peppermint extract**
- 3 **drops green food coloring**

TOPPING
- 1½ **cups milk chocolate chips**
- 6 **tablespoons butter, softened**
- ¼ **teaspoon peppermint extract**

1. Prepare the cake according to package directions, using a greased 15x10x1-in. baking pan.

2. Bake at 350° for 25-30 minutes or until a toothpick inserted near the center comes out clean. Cool on a wire rack.

3. In a large bowl, combine the frosting ingredients until smooth. Spread over cooled cake.

4. For topping, in a microwave, melt chocolate chips and butter; stir until smooth. Stir in extract. Spread over frosting. Refrigerate until set.

ORANGE-COLA CHOCOLATE CAKE

Substituting cola for water, adding a hint of orange flavor and serving each slice with dipped strawberries turns a simple mix into a spectacular dessert people love!

—STEPHANIE VOGEL LINCOLN, NE

PREP: 25 MIN. • **BAKE:** 30 MIN. + COOLING • **MAKES:** 12 SERVINGS

1 **package devil's food cake mix (regular size)**
- 3 **eggs**
- 1⅓ **cups cola**
- ½ **cup canola oil**
- 1 **tablespoon orange extract**

CHOCOLATE-COVERED STRAWBERRIES
- ½ **cup semisweet chocolate chips**
- 1 **teaspoon shortening**
- 12 **fresh strawberries**

FROSTING
- ½ **cup butter, softened**
- 3¾ **cups confectioners' sugar**

- 3 **tablespoons instant chocolate drink mix**
- ¼ **cup cola**
- ½ **teaspoon orange extract**

1. In a large bowl, combine cake mix, eggs, cola, oil and extract. Beat on low speed for 30 seconds; beat on medium for 2 minutes. Pour into a greased 13x9-in. baking pan.

2. Bake at 350° for 30-35 minutes or until a toothpick inserted near the center comes out clean. Cool on a wire rack.

3. In a small microwave-safe bowl, melt chocolate chips and shortening; stir until smooth. Wash strawberries and pat dry. Dip each strawberry into chocolate; allow excess to drip off. Place on a waxed paper-lined baking sheet; refrigerate until set, about 30 minutes.

4. In a small bowl, combine the frosting ingredients; beat until smooth. Frost cake. Garnish each serving with a chocolate-covered strawberry.

NOTE *Diet cola is not recommended for this recipe.*

UPSIDE-DOWN BERRY CAKE

This cake is good warm or cold and served with whipped topping or ice cream.
It's very moist with loads of flavor and can be whipped up in just minutes. Enjoy!
—**CANDICE SCHOLL** WEST SUNBURY, PA

PREP: 20 MIN. • **BAKE:** 30 MIN. + COOLING • **MAKES:** 15 SERVINGS

½ cup chopped walnuts
1 cup fresh or frozen blueberries
1 cup fresh or frozen raspberries, halved
1 cup sliced fresh strawberries
¼ cup sugar
1 package (3 ounces) raspberry gelatin
1 package yellow cake mix (regular size)
2 eggs
1¼ cups water
2 tablespoons canola oil
1½ cups miniature marshmallows

1. In a well greased 13x9-in. baking pan, layer the walnuts and berries; sprinkle with sugar and gelatin. In a large bowl, combine the cake mix, eggs, water and oil; beat on low speed for 30 seconds. Beat on medium for 2 minutes. Fold in marshmallows. Pour over top.

2. Bake at 350° for 35-40 minutes or until a toothpick inserted near the center comes out clean. Cool for 5 minutes before inverting onto a serving platter. Store in the refrigerator.

WHITE CHOCOLATE FUDGE CAKE

Here's a sweet cake with thick frosting and a rich chocolate layer. It's a big hit at office potlucks.
I have one co-worker who tells everyone it's awful so he can have it all to himself!

—DENISE VONSTEIN SHILOH, OH

PREP: 25 MIN. + COOLING • **BAKE:** 25 MIN. • **MAKES:** 16 SERVINGS

- 1 package white cake mix (regular size)
- 1¼ cups water
- 3 egg whites
- ⅓ cup canola oil
- 1 teaspoon vanilla extract
- 3 ounces white baking chocolate, melted

FILLING
- ¾ cup semisweet chocolate chips
- 2 tablespoons butter

FROSTING
- 1 can (16 ounces) vanilla frosting
- 3 ounces white baking chocolate, melted
- 1 teaspoon vanilla extract
- 1 carton (8 ounces) frozen whipped topping, thawed

1. In a large bowl, combine the cake mix, water, egg whites, oil and vanilla. Beat on low for 30 seconds. Beat on medium for 2 minutes. Stir in white chocolate. Pour into a greased 13x9-in. baking pan.

2. Bake at 350° for 25-30 minutes or until a toothpick inserted near the center comes out clean. Cool for 5 minutes.

3. Meanwhile, in a microwave-safe dish, microwave chocolate chips and butter until melted; stir until smooth. Carefully spread over warm cake. Cool completely.

4. In a small bowl, beat frosting until fluffy; beat in the white chocolate and vanilla until smooth. Fold in the whipped topping; frost the cake. Store in the refrigerator.

LIGHT PEANUT BUTTER CHOCOLATE CAKE

When my mom was told to avoid sugar and fats, I whipped up this light, delectable dessert for her.
She loves indulging her sweet tooth while following doctor's orders.

—ANNETTE ABBOTT CHARLOTTE, NC

PREP: 25 MIN. • **BAKE:** 20 MIN. + COOLING • **MAKES:** 18 SERVINGS

1 **package devil's food cake mix (regular size)**
1 **cup water**
3 **eggs**
⅓ **cup unsweetened applesauce**
¼ **cup reduced-fat creamy peanut butter**
FROSTING
½ **cup cold fat-free milk**
1 **package (1.4 ounces) sugar-free instant chocolate pudding mix**
1 **package (8 ounces) reduced-fat cream cheese**
½ **cup reduced-fat creamy peanut butter**

1 **carton (8 ounces) frozen reduced-fat whipped topping, thawed**

1. In a large bowl, combine cake mix, water, eggs and applesauce. Beat on low speed for 30 seconds. Beat on medium speed for 2 minutes. Transfer to a 13x9-in. baking dish coated with cooking spray.

2. Bake at 350° for 30-35 minutes or until a toothpick inserted near the center comes out clean.

3. Immediately drop small amounts of peanut butter over hot cake; return to the oven for 1 minute. Carefully spread peanut butter over cake. Cool on a wire rack.

4. For frosting, in a small bowl, whisk milk and pudding mix for 1 minute. In a small bowl, beat cream cheese and peanut butter until smooth. Gradually beat in the pudding. Beat in half of the whipped topping; fold in the remaining whipped topping. Frost the cake. Store in the refrigerator.

CHOCOLATE CANNOLI CAKE ROLL

Creamy ricotta cheese filling with a hint of cinnamon rolls up beautifully in this fluffy chocolate cake.

—TAMMY REX, NEW TRIPOLI, PENNSYLVANIA

PREP: 20 MIN. + CHILLING • **BAKE:** 15 MIN. + COOLING • **MAKES:** 12 SERVINGS

1¾ cups chocolate cake mix
⅓ cup water
2 tablespoons canola oil
3 eggs

FILLING

1 package (8 ounces) cream cheese, softened
2 cups ricotta cheese
1 cup confectioners' sugar
1 teaspoon vanilla extract
½ teaspoon ground cinnamon
½ cup miniature semisweet chocolate chips

1. Line a greased 15x10x1-in. baking pan with waxed paper and grease the paper; set aside. In a large bowl, combine the cake mix, water, oil and eggs; beat on low speed for 30 seconds. Beat on medium for 2 minutes. Pour into prepared pan.

2. Bake at 350° for 12-14 minutes or until cake springs back when lightly touched. Cool 5 minutes. Invert onto a kitchen towel dusted with confectioners' sugar. Gently peel off waxed paper. Roll up cake in the towel jelly-roll style, starting with a short side. Cool completely on a wire rack.

3. In a bowl, beat cream cheese until fluffy. Add ricotta cheese, confectioners' sugar, vanilla and cinnamon; beat until smooth. Stir in chips. Unroll cake; spread filling over cake to within ½ in. of edges. Roll up again. Place seam side down on a serving platter. Refrigerate for 2 hours before serving. Store in the refrigerator.

TOFFEE POKE CAKE

This recipe is a favorite among family and friends. I enjoy making it because it is so simple.
The luscious caramel tastes wonderful with the chocolate cake.

—JEANETTE HOFFMAN OSHKOSH, WI

PREP: 25 MIN. • **BAKE:** 25 MIN. + CHILLING • **MAKES:** 15 SERVINGS

- 1 **package chocolate cake mix (regular size)**
- 1 **jar (17 ounces) butterscotch-caramel ice cream topping**
- 1 **carton (12 ounces) frozen whipped topping, thawed**
- 3 **Heath candy bars (1.4 ounces each), chopped**

1. Prepare and bake the cake according to package directions, using a greased 13x9-in. baking pan. Cool on a wire rack.
2. Using the handle of a wooden spoon, poke holes in cake. Pour ¾ cup caramel topping into holes. Spoon remaining caramel over cake. Top with whipped topping. Sprinkle with candy. Refrigerate for at least 2 hours before serving.

FAST FIX ▶ PINEAPPLE UPSIDE-DOWN CAKE

It takes just 10 minutes to whip up my cake recipe...and it's finished
when it comes out of the oven since there's no frosting.

—KAREN ANN BLAND GOVE, KS

PREP: 10 MIN. • **BAKE:** 45 MIN. • **MAKES:** 12-15 SERVINGS

- ¼ **cup butter, melted**
- 1 **can (20 ounces) sliced pineapple**
- 10 **pecan halves**
- 1 **jar (12 ounces) apricot preserves**
- 1 **package yellow cake mix (regular size)**

1. Pour butter into a well-greased 13x9-in. baking dish. Drain pineapple, reserving ¼ cup juice. Arrange pineapple slices in prepared pan; place a pecan half in the center of each slice. Combine the apricot preserves and reserved pineapple juice; spoon over pineapple slices.

2. Prepare cake batter according to package directions; pour over pineapple.
3. Bake at 350° for 45-50 minutes or until a toothpick inserted near the center comes out clean. Immediately invert onto a large serving platter. Cool slightly; serve warm.

BUTTERSCOTCH CHOCOLATE CAKE

This cake can be made ahead. Moist cake is covered with rich butterscotch
ice cream topping, whipped topping and crushed candy bars.

—SHELLEY MCKINNEY NEW CASTLE, IN

PREP: 10 MIN. + CHILLING • **BAKE:** 30 MIN. + CHILLING • **MAKES:** 12-16 SERVINGS

- **1 package chocolate cake mix (regular size)**
- **1 jar (17 ounces) butterscotch ice cream topping**
- **1 carton (8 ounces) frozen whipped topping, thawed**
- **3 Butterfinger candy bars (2.1 ounces each), coarsely crushed**

1. Prepare and bake the cake according to package directions, using a greased 13x9-in. baking pan. Cool on a wire rack for 30 minutes.

2. Using the end of a wooden spoon handle, poke 12 holes in warm cake. Pour butterscotch topping over cake; cool completely.

3. Spread with whipped topping; sprinkle with candy. Refrigerate for at least 2 hours before serving. Store in the refrigerator.

FAST FIX ▸ **RICH BUTTER CAKE**

I've been bringing this cake to family get-togethers and church meetings for a very long time. The scrumptious standby, topped with cream cheese and nuts, can be prepared in a wink.

—**DORIS SCHLOEMAN** CHICAGO, IL

PREP: 15 MIN. • **BAKE:** 35 MIN.
MAKES: 12-15 SERVINGS

- 1 **package (16 ounces) pound cake mix**
- ½ **cup butter, melted**
- 5 **eggs**
- 2 **cups confectioners' sugar, divided**
- 2 **packages (one 8 ounces, one 3 ounces) cream cheese, softened**
- ½ **teaspoon vanilla extract**
- 1 **cup chopped walnuts**

1. In a large bowl, combine the cake mix, butter and 3 eggs; beat until smooth. Spread into a greased 13x9-in. baking pan.

2. Set aside 2 tablespoons confectioners' sugar for topping. In a large bowl, beat the cream cheese, vanilla and remaining confectioners' sugar until smooth. Beat in remaining eggs. Pour over batter. Sprinkle with the walnuts.

3. Bake at 350° for 35-40 minutes or until a toothpick inserted near the center comes out clean. Cool on a wire rack. Dust with reserved confectioners' sugar. Store in the refrigerator.

LIGHTENED-UP PECAN UPSIDE-DOWN CAKE

My dessert is packed with pecans and sweetness. Using reduced-fat ingredients
makes it a lighter choice if you're counting calories.

—MAE JOHNSON DE RIDDER, LA

PREP: 20 MIN. • **BAKE:** 30 MIN. + COOLING • **MAKES:** 20 SERVINGS

- ½ **cup reduced-fat butter,
  melted**
- ½ **cup packed brown sugar**
- ¼ **cup dark corn syrup**
- 1½ **cups pecan halves**
- 1 **package butter pecan cake
  mix (regular size)**
- 1 **cup reduced-fat sour cream**
- ⅓ **cup unsweetened applesauce**
- 2 **eggs**
- 2 **egg whites**
- 1 **teaspoon vanilla extract**

1. In a small bowl, combine the butter, brown sugar, corn syrup and pecans. Spread evenly into a 13x9-in. baking pan coated with cooking spray. Set aside.

2. In a large bowl, combine the remaining ingredients; beat on low speed for 30 seconds. Beat on medium for 2 minutes. Transfer to prepared pan.

3. Bake at 350° for 30-35 minutes or until a toothpick inserted near the center comes out clean. Cool for 5 minutes before inverting onto a serving platter. Serve warm or at room temperature.

NOTE *This recipe was tested with Land O'Lakes light stick butter.*

STRAWBERRY SHORTCAKE DESSERT

A co-worker shared this recipe with me. I've used other fruits, including blueberries, cherries and peaches for the shortcake, and it always gets fabulous comments.

—MICHELE TRACHIER PASADENA, TX

PREP: 10 MIN. • **BAKE:** 30 MIN. + CHILLING • **MAKES:** 20 SERVINGS

1 **package white cake mix (regular size)**
1⅓ **cups water**
¼ **cup unsweetened applesauce**
2 **egg whites**
1 **egg**
1 **package (.6 ounce) sugar-free strawberry gelatin**
2 **cups boiling water**
1 **package (16 ounces) frozen unsweetened whole strawberries, thawed, drained and sliced**
1 **carton (16 ounces) frozen reduced-fat whipped topping, thawed**
10 **fresh strawberries, halved**

1. In a large bowl, combine the cake mix, water, applesauce, egg whites and egg; beat on low speed for 30 seconds. Beat on medium for 2 minutes. Pour into a 13x9-in. baking dish coated with cooking spray.

2. Bake at 350° for 30-35 minutes or until a toothpick inserted near the center comes out clean.

3. In a large bowl, dissolve gelatin in boiling water. Stir in the strawberries. Using a sharp knife, make a diamond pattern in the top of the hot cake; immediately pour gelatin mixture over cake. Cool on a wire rack.

4. Refrigerate for at least 6 hours. Spread with whipped topping. Garnish with fresh strawberries.

FAST FIX ROOT BEER FLOAT CAKE

Serve this cake to a bunch of hungry kids and watch it disappear!
I put root beer in both the cake portion and the fluffy, irresistible topping. Yum.

—KAT THOMPSON PRINEVILLE, OR

PREP: 15 MIN. • **BAKE:** 30 MIN. + COOLING • **MAKES:** 12-15 SERVINGS

1 package white cake mix
   (regular size)
1¾ cups cold root beer, divided
¼ cup canola oil
2 eggs
1 envelope whipped topping
   mix (Dream Whip)

1. In a large bowl, combine the cake mix, 1¼ cups root beer, oil and eggs. Beat on low speed for 2 minutes or stir by hand for 3 minutes. Pour into a greased 13x9-in. baking pan.
2. Bake at 350° for 30-35 minutes or until a toothpick inserted near the center comes out clean. Cool completely on a wire rack.

3. In a small bowl, combine the whipped topping mix and remaining root beer. Beat until soft peaks form. Frost cake. Store in the refrigerator.

FAST FIX CARAMEL-FUDGE CHOCOLATE CAKE

To satisfy the chocolate lovers in our family, I added hot fudge topping and chocolate chips to a caramel-covered
dessert that's quite popular in our area. The rich toppings make it especially decadent.

—KAREN STUCKY FREEMAN, SD

PREP: 15 MIN. • **BAKE:** 35 MIN. + COOLING • **MAKES:** 12-15 SERVINGS

1 package chocolate cake mix
   (regular size)
1 cup miniature semisweet
   chocolate chips, divided
1 jar (12¼ ounces) caramel ice
   cream topping, warmed
1 jar (11¾ ounces) hot fudge ice
   cream topping, warmed
1 carton (8 ounces) frozen
   whipped topping, thawed

½ cup English toffee bits or
   almond brickle chips

1. Prepare cake batter according to the package directions. Stir in ¾ cup chocolate chips. Pour into a greased 13x9-in. baking pan.
2. Bake at 350° for 35-40 minutes or until a toothpick inserted in center comes out clean.

3. Immediately poke holes in the cake with a meat fork or skewer. Spread caramel and fudge toppings over cake. Cool on a wire rack.
4. Frost with whipped topping. Sprinkle with toffee bits and remaining chocolate chips. Store in the refrigerator.

APPLE GERMAN CHOCOLATE CAKE

This awesome dessert is perfect to bake when unexpected guests stop by. Cake mix and canned pie filling come together to make the snack cake a cinch to assemble, while chocolate chips and nuts create the wonderful topping.

—SHIRLEY WEAVER ZEELAND, MI

PREP: 15 MIN. • **BAKE:** 40 MIN. • **MAKES:** 12-15 SERVINGS

- **1 can (21 ounces) apple pie filling**
- **1 package German chocolate cake mix (regular size)**
- **3 eggs**
- **¾ cup coarsely chopped walnuts**
- **½ cup miniature semisweet chocolate chips**

1. Place pie filling in a blender; cover and process until apples are in ¼-in. chunks. Pour into a large bowl; add cake mix and eggs. Beat on medium speed for 5 minutes.

Pour into a greased 13-in. x 9-in. baking pan. Sprinkle with nuts and chocolate chips.

2. Bake at 350° for 40-45 minutes or until a toothpick inserted near the center comes out clean. Cool completely on a wire rack before cutting.

GRANDMA'S LEMON POPPY SEED CAKE

I found the cake recipe in a collection of family recipes. My granddaughter, Riley, likes that it tastes like lemons and is refreshingly sweet. It's always wonderful.

—PHYLLIS HARMON NELSON, WI

PREP: 20 MIN.
BAKE: 30 MIN. + COOLING
MAKES: 15 SERVINGS

- 1 **package lemon cake mix (regular size)**
- 1 **package (3.4 ounces) instant vanilla pudding mix**
- 4 **eggs**
- 1 **cup water**
- ½ **cup canola oil**
- ¼ **cup poppy seeds**

DRIZZLE

- 2 **cups confectioners' sugar**
- 2 **tablespoons water**
- 2 **tablespoons lemon juice**

1. In a large bowl, combine the cake mix, pudding mix, eggs, water and oil; beat on low speed for 30 seconds. Beat on medium for 2 minutes. Fold in the poppy seeds. Transfer to a greased and floured 13x9-in. baking pan.

2. Bake at 350° for 30-35 minutes or until a toothpick inserted near the center comes out clean. Cool on a wire rack.

3. For drizzle, in a small bowl, combine the confectioners' sugar, water and lemon juice; drizzle over cake.

EGGNOG TRES LECHES CAKE

When the holidays roll around, my family eagerly anticipates sampling
my eggnog cake. Its rich seasonal flavor is something to celebrate!

—JAN VALDEZ CHICAGO, IL

PREP: 40 MIN. + STANDING • **BAKE:** 25 MIN. + CHILLING • **MAKES:** 15 SERVINGS

- 1 **package white cake mix (regular size)**
- 1⅓ **cups water**
- 2 **tablespoons canola oil**
- 3 **egg whites**
- 2 **cups eggnog**
- 1 **can (14 ounces) sweetened condensed milk**
- ½ **cup 2% milk**
- 1½ **cups heavy whipping cream**
- ¼ **cup sugar**
- ⅛ **teaspoon ground cinnamon**
- ⅛ **teaspoon ground nutmeg**

1. In a large bowl, combine the cake mix, water, oil and egg whites; beat on low speed for 30 seconds. Beat on medium for 2 minutes. Pour into a greased and floured 13x9-in. baking pan.

2. Bake at 350° for 25-30 minutes or until a toothpick inserted near the center comes out clean. Cool on a wire rack. Using a skewer, poke holes in cake 1 in. apart.

3. In a large bowl, combine the eggnog, sweetened condensed milk and 2% milk. Pour a scant ¾ cup mixture over cake; let stand for 20-30 minutes or until liquid is absorbed. Repeat four times. Cover and refrigerate for 8 hours or overnight.

4. In a large bowl, beat cream until it begins to thicken. Add sugar; beat until soft peaks form. Spread over cake. Sprinkle with the cinnamon and nutmeg. Refrigerate leftovers.

NOTE *This recipe was tested with commercially prepared eggnog.*

FAST FIX # SLOW COOKER CHOCOLATE LAVA CAKE

Everyone who tries this dessert falls in love with it. Using a slow cooker liner makes cleanup a breeze.

—LATONA DWYER PALM BEACH GARDENS, FL

PREP: 15 MIN. • **COOK:** 3 HOURS • **MAKES:** 12 SERVINGS

- 1 package devil's food cake mix (regular size)
- 1⅔ cups water
- 3 eggs
- ⅓ cup canola oil
- 2 cups cold 2% milk
- 1 package (3.9 ounces) instant chocolate pudding mix
- 2 cups (12 ounces) semisweet chocolate chips

1. In a large bowl, combine the cake mix, water, eggs and oil; beat on low speed for 30 seconds. Beat on medium for 2 minutes. Pour into a greased 4-qt. slow cooker.

2. In another bowl, whisk milk and pudding mix for 2 minutes. Let stand for 2 minutes or until soft-set. Spoon over cake batter; sprinkle with chocolate chips.

3. Cover and cook on high for 3-4 hours or until a toothpick inserted in cake portion comes out with moist crumbs. Serve warm. Refrigerate leftovers.

LEMON CAKE

With a refreshing lemon glaze, this fluffy cake is full of citrus flavor but not much fat or cholesterol.

—BONITA GIESBRECHT GLENN, CA

PREP: 20 MIN. • **BAKE:** 25 MIN. + COOLING • **MAKES:** 15 SERVINGS

- 1 package white cake mix (regular size)
- 1 package (3 ounces) lemon gelatin
- 1 cup plus 2 tablespoons water
- 4 egg whites
- ⅓ cup unsweetened applesauce
- 1 tablespoon canola oil
- 1 teaspoon lemon extract
- 4 drops yellow food coloring, optional

LEMON GLAZE
- 1½ cups confectioners' sugar
- ⅓ cup lemon juice

1. In a large bowl, combine the cake mix, gelatin, water, egg whites, applesauce, oil, lemon extract and food coloring if desired; beat on low speed for 30 seconds. Beat on medium for 2 minutes. Pour into a 13x9-in. baking pan coated with cooking spray.

2. Bake at 350° for 25-30 minutes or until edges are lightly browned and a toothpick inserted near center comes out clean. Cool on a wire rack for 10 minutes.

3. Meanwhile, for glaze, in a bowl, combine confectioners' sugar and lemon juice until smooth. Drizzle about a third of the glaze over cake; carefully spread evenly. Repeat with the remaining glaze. Cool completely.

BANANA CAKE

You don't even need ripe bananas to whip up this easy-to-make banana cake.

—PATSY HOOD NEMO, SD

PREP: 20 MIN. • **BAKE:** 30 MIN. + COOLING • **MAKES:** 12-16 SERVINGS

- 1 package yellow cake mix (regular size)
- 1 package (3.4 ounces) instant banana pudding mix
- 1¼ cups water
- ⅓ cup canola oil
- 2 eggs
- 2 teaspoons banana extract
  Frosting of your choice

1. Line a 13x9-in. baking pan with waxed paper; grease and flour paper. Set aside.

2. In a large bowl, combine the cake and pudding mixes, water, oil, eggs and extract. Beat on low speed for 1 minute or until moistened; beat on medium for 4 minutes. Pour batter into prepared pan.

3. Bake at 350° for 30-35 minutes or until a toothpick inserted near the center comes out clean. Cool for 10 minutes before removing from pan to a wire rack to cool completely. Frost the cake.

NOTE *Banana extract is available at cake decorating and candy supply stores.*

FAST FIX ▸ YUM-YUM CAKE

This cake has been a family favorite ever since my mom received the recipe from a neighbor.
My husband's co-workers ask him to bring this cake for his birthday treat every year.

—**TERESA MARCHESE** NEW BERLIN, WI

PREP: 15 MIN. • **BAKE:** 20 MIN. + COOLING • **MAKES:** 12-16 SERVINGS

1½ **cups cold milk**
1 **package (3.4 ounces) instant vanilla pudding mix**
1 **package white or yellow cake mix (regular size)**
1½ **cups whipped topping**
1 **can (8 ounces) crushed pineapple, well drained**
¼ **cup flaked coconut, toasted**

1. In a small bowl, whisk milk and pudding mix for 2 minutes. Let stand for 2 minutes or until soft-set; cover and refrigerate.
2. Grease the bottom of two 8-in. square baking dishes. Prepare cake batter according to package directions; pour into prepared dishes.
3. Bake at 350° for 20-25 minutes or until a toothpick inserted near the center comes out clean. Cool for 10 minutes before removing from pans to wire racks to cool completely.
4. Fold whipped topping into pudding until blended. Level cake tops if necessary. Place one cake on a serving plate; spread with half of the pudding mixture. Top with pineapple, and remaining cake and pudding mixture. Sprinkle with coconut. Store in the refrigerator.

{5}

Angel Food Cakes

140

Double Berry Lemon Dessert

144

Orange-Coconut Angel Food Cake

147

Apricot-Raspberry Angel Torte

HEAVENLY ANGEL FOOD CAKE

Five ingredients are all you'll need to whip up this impressive layer cake featuring a chocolaty filling. Soft and airy, each slice melts in your mouth.

—TERI ROBERTS HILLIARD, OH

PREP: 20 MIN.
BAKE: 35 MIN. + CHILLING
MAKES: 12 SERVINGS

- 1 package (16 ounces) angel food cake mix
- 24 large marshmallows
- 6 milk chocolate candy bars with almonds (1.45 ounces each), chopped
- ⅔ cup milk
- 1 carton (12 ounces) frozen whipped topping, thawed, divided

1. Prepare and bake the cake according to package directions, using an ungreased 10-in. tube pan. Immediately invert pan; cool completely, about 1 hour. Run a knife around side and center tube of pan. Remove cake from pan.
2. For filling, in a small saucepan, combine marshmallows, candy bars and milk. Cook and stir over low heat until marshmallows are melted. Transfer to a small bowl; cool to room temperature. Fold in ¾ cup whipped topping.
3. Cut cake horizontally into three layers. Place bottom layer on a serving plate; spread with a third of filling. Repeat layers twice. Chill for at least 1 hour.
4. Frost top and sides of cake with remaining whipped topping. Store in the refrigerator.

ORANGE-ANGEL JELLY ROLL

I came up with this orange dessert just in time for Easter. Everyone agreed the flavor reminded them of a zesty, creamy Dreamsicle. It was a definite hit!

—MICHELLE TOKARZ NEWPORT, MI

PREP: 25 MIN. • **BAKE:** 20 MIN. + COOLING • **MAKES:** 12 SERVINGS

- 1 **package (16 ounces) angel food cake mix**
- 1 **package (8 ounces) cream cheese, softened**
- ¼ **cup confectioners' sugar**
- 1 **tablespoon orange juice**
- ½ **teaspoon orange extract**
- ½ **teaspoon grated orange peel**
- 3 **drops yellow food coloring, optional**
- 1 **drop red food coloring, optional**
- 1 **cup whipped topping**
- ⅔ **cup orange marmalade**
  Additional confectioners' sugar and orange curls

1. Line a greased 15x10x1-in. baking pan with waxed paper; grease the paper and set aside. Prepare the cake mix batter according to package directions; spread evenly into prepared pan.

2. Bake at 350° for 18-22 minutes or until cake springs back when lightly touched. Cool in pan for 5 minutes. Carefully run a knife around the edges of the pan to loosen cake. Invert onto a kitchen towel dusted with confectioners' sugar. Gently peel off waxed paper. Roll up cake in the towel jelly-roll style, starting with a short side. Cool completely on a wire rack.

3. For filling, in a small bowl, beat cream cheese and confectioners' sugar until smooth. Beat in the orange juice, orange extract, orange peel and food coloring if desired. Fold in whipped topping.

4. Unroll the cake; spread the marmalade to within ½ in. of edges. Spread whipped topping mixture over marmalade to within 1 in. of edges. Roll up again. Place seam side down on a serving platter. Sprinkle with additional confectioners' sugar. Garnish with the orange curls. Store in the refrigerator.

DOUBLE BERRY LEMON DESSERT

When my neighbor gave me a bowl of blackberries, I took to the kitchen and created this recipe.
My mother is diabetic and loves it.

—VICKI MELIES ELKHORN, NE

PREP: 25 MIN. • **BAKE:** 20 MIN. + COOLING • **MAKES:** 8 SERVINGS

1⅓ cups angel food cake mix
⅔ cup cold water
1 cup cold 2% milk
1 package (1 ounce) sugar-free instant lemon pudding mix
1 package (8 ounces) reduced-fat cream cheese
½ cup fresh or frozen raspberries
½ cup fresh or frozen blackberries
1 teaspoon sugar

1. In a small bowl, combine the cake mix and water; beat on low speed for 30 seconds. Beat on medium for 1 minute. Pour into an ungreased 11x7-in. baking pan. Bake at 350° for 20-25 minutes or until golden brown and entire top appears dry. Cool completely, about 40 minutes.

2. In a small bowl, whisk milk and pudding mix. In a small bowl, beat cream cheese until smooth; beat in pudding mixture until blended. Run a knife around sides of pan. Remove the cake and cut horizontally into two layers. Place bottom layer on a serving plate; spread with half of the pudding mixture. Top with remaining cake layer and pudding mixture.

3. In a small bowl, combine the raspberries, blackberries and sugar. Serve with the cake. Store in the refrigerator.

PEPPERMINT CAKE ROLLS

With angel food cake, fudge sauce and peppermints, this cake roll is easy and pretty.
—SUELLEN CALHOUN DES MOINES, IA

PREP: 25 MIN. • **BAKE:** 15 MIN + COOLING • **MAKES:** 2 CAKES (10 SLICES EACH)

1 **package (16 ounces) angel food cake mix**
   Confectioners' sugar
1 **carton (16 ounces) frozen whipped topping, thawed**
1½ **teaspoons peppermint extract**
1 **cup hot fudge ice cream topping**
½ **cup crushed peppermint candies, divided**
   Fresh mint leaves, optional

1. Line two greased 15x10x1-in. baking pans with waxed paper. Prepare cake mix according to package directions. Divide the batter evenly into prepared pans, spreading evenly.
2. Bake at 350° for 12-15 minutes or until tops spring back when lightly touched. Cool 5 minutes.
3. Invert each cake onto a kitchen towel dusted with confectioners' sugar. Gently peel off paper. Roll up cake in the towel jelly-roll style, starting with a short side. Cool completely on a wire rack.
4. In a small bowl, mix whipped topping and extract until blended. Unroll cakes; spread each with 1½ cups peppermint mixture to within ½ in. of edges.
5. Cut a small hole in the corner of a food-safe plastic bag; fill with fudge topping. Drizzle each cake with half of the fudge topping; sprinkle with 2 tablespoons crushed candies. Roll up again, without towel.
6. Transfer to platters. Frost with remaining peppermint mixture. Cakes can be served immediately or frozen, covered, for later use. Remove from the freezer 10 minutes before serving. Top with remaining candies and, if desired, mint leaves just before serving.

SNOWBALL CAKE

I couldn't pry this family secret recipe from my sister-in-law, but her mother did…and I was thrilled when she gave me a copy! The old-fashioned flavor never goes out of style.

—NORMA WEHRUNG GETZVILLE, NY

PREP: 25 MIN. • **BAKE:** 40 MIN. + CHILLING • **MAKES:** 20 SERVINGS

- 1 **package (16 ounces) angel food cake mix**
- 2 **envelopes unflavored gelatin**
- ¼ **cup cold water**
- 1 **cup boiling water**
- 1 **can (20 ounces) crushed pineapple, undrained**
- 1 **cup sugar**
- 3 **tablespoons lemon juice**
- ¼ **teaspoon salt**
- 4 **envelopes whipped topping mix (Dream Whip)**
- 2 **cups milk**
  Toasted flaked coconut and maraschino cherries

1. Prepare and bake the cake according to package directions, using an ungreased 10-in. tube pan. Immediately invert pan; cool completely, about 1 hour.

2. Meanwhile, in a large bowl, sprinkle gelatin over cold water; let stand for 1 minute. Stir in boiling water until gelatin is dissolved. Add the pineapple, sugar, lemon juice and salt. Refrigerate until partially thickened, about 40 minutes.

3. In a large bowl, beat whipped topping mixes and milk until stiff. Fold into pineapple mixture.

4. Run a knife around sides and center tube of cake pan; remove cake from pan and cut into 1-in. cubes. Place half of the cake cubes in a 13x9-in. dish; top with half of the filling. Repeat the layers. Refrigerate for at least 1 hour.

5. Sprinkle with coconut. Cut into squares; top each with a cherry. Store in the refrigerator.

ANGEL FOOD CAKE ROLL

There's always room for dessert—especially when it's this eye-catching frozen fare. We like strawberry yogurt in the filling, but different flavors work well, too. My make-ahead treat is also my most-requested.
—JOAN COLBERT SIGOURNEY, IA

PREP: 20 MIN. • **BAKE:** 15 MIN. + FREEZING • **MAKES:** 10 SERVINGS

- 1 **package (16 ounces) angel food cake mix**
- 5 **teaspoons confectioners' sugar**
- 1 **cup (8 ounces) strawberry yogurt**
- 1 **package (1 ounce) instant sugar-free vanilla pudding mix**
- 3 **drops red food coloring, optional**
- 2 **cups reduced-fat whipped topping**

1. Line a 15x10x1-in. baking pan with waxed paper. Prepare cake batter according to package directions. Pour batter into the prepared pan.

2. Bake at 350° for 15-20 minutes or until the cake springs back when lightly touched. Cool for 5 minutes.

3. Carefully run a knife around the edges of the pan. Turn cake onto a kitchen towel dusted with confectioners' sugar. Gently peel off waxed paper. Roll up jelly-roll style in the towel, starting with a short side. Cool on a wire rack.

4. In a large bowl, whisk the yogurt, pudding mix and food coloring if desired. Fold in the whipped topping.

5. Unroll cake; spread filling evenly over cake to within ½ in. of edges. Roll up. Cover and freeze. Remove from freezer 30 minutes before slicing. Store in the freezer.

ORANGE-COCONUT ANGEL FOOD CAKE

Everyone who tries this luscious cake loves it—the filling, the light topping, every bit!
I have several cake recipes, but this is my favorite to make and eat!

—BETTY KINSER ELIZABETHTON, TN

PREP: 25 MIN. • **BAKE:** 30 MIN. + COOLING • **MAKES:** 14 SERVINGS

- 1 **package (16 ounces) angel food cake mix**
- 1 **cup cold water**
- ⅓ **cup orange juice**
- 2 **teaspoons orange extract, divided**
- 1¾ **cups cold fat-free milk**
- 1 **package (1 ounce) sugar-free instant vanilla pudding mix**
- 1 **tablespoon grated orange peel**
- 1¼ **cups flaked coconut, divided**
- 1 **carton (8 ounces) frozen reduced-fat whipped topping, thawed, divided**

1. In a large bowl, combine the cake mix, water, orange juice and 1 teaspoon orange extract. Beat on low speed for 30 seconds. Beat on medium for 2 minutes. Spoon into an ungreased 10-in. tube pan.

2. Bake cake on the lowest oven rack position at 375° for 30-35 minutes or until lightly browned and entire top appears dry. Immediately invert pan; cool completely, about 1 hour. Run a knife around side and center tube of pan. Remove cake from pan.

3. In a small bowl, whisk milk and pudding mix for 2 minutes.

Stir in the orange peel and the remaining orange extract. Let stand for 2 minutes or until soft-set. Fold in ¾ cup coconut and ¾ cup whipped topping.

4. Split the cake into three horizontal layers. Place bottom layer on a serving plate; top with half of the pudding mixture. Repeat the layers. Top with the remaining cake layer. Frost top and sides of cake with remaining whipped topping. Toast the remaining coconut; sprinkle over top and sides of cake. Store in the refrigerator.

FAST FIX ▶ RASPBERRY ANGEL CAKE

Not only is this an uplifting dessert, but it's virtually fat-free and has no cholesterol.
Best of all, it's a delicious, tart treat that comes together easily.

—SHERI ERICKSON MONTROSE, IA

PREP: 15 MIN. • **BAKE:** 45 MIN. + COOLING • **MAKES:** 12 SERVINGS

- 1 **package (16 ounces) angel food cake mix**
- ½ **teaspoon almond extract**
- ½ **teaspoon vanilla extract**
- 1 **package (.3 ounce) sugar-free raspberry gelatin**
- 1 **package (12 ounces) frozen unsweetened raspberries, thawed**
- 1 **tablespoon sugar**

1. Prepare cake batter according to package directions. Fold in extracts. Spoon two-thirds of the batter into an ungreased 10-in. tube pan. Add gelatin powder to remaining batter; drop by tablespoonfuls over batter in pan. Cut through with a knife to swirl.

2. Bake the cake according to package directions. Immediately invert pan; cool completely, about 1 hour. Run a knife around side and center tube of pan. Remove cake from pan. Cut into slices.

3. Combine raspberries and sugar; serve with cake.

FRUITY COCONUT CAKE ROLL

Kiwi and coconut add tropical flair to this moist, fruity and simply delicious dessert.
It makes a light, refreshing and stunning finale to even the fanciest meal!

—NANCY GRANAMAN BURLINGTON, IA

PREP: 30 MIN. • **BAKE:** 20 MIN. + CHILLING • **MAKES:** 12 SERVINGS

- 1 **package (16 ounces) angel food cake mix**
- ½ **teaspoon plus 3 tablespoons confectioners' sugar, divided**
- ¾ **cup cold fat-free milk**
- 1 **package (1 ounce) sugar-free instant white chocolate pudding mix**
- 1 **carton (8 ounces) frozen fat-free whipped topping, thawed**
- ½ **teaspoon coconut extract**
- 2 **medium kiwifruit, peeled and thinly sliced**
- 2 **cups fresh strawberries, sliced**
- ⅓ **cup plus 2 tablespoons flaked coconut, divided**
- 2 **tablespoons apricot spreadable fruit**
- ½ **teaspoon hot water**

1. Line a 15x10x1-in. baking pan with waxed paper; coat the paper with cooking spray and set aside. Prepare cake batter according to package directions. Spread evenly in prepared pan.

2. Bake at 350° for 16-20 minutes or until golden brown. Carefully run a knife around the edges of the pan. Turn cake onto a kitchen towel dusted with ½ teaspoon confectioners' sugar. Gently peel off waxed paper. Dust with the remaining confectioners' sugar. Roll up cake in the towel jelly-roll style, starting with a short side. Cool completely on a wire rack.

3. For filling, in a large bowl, whisk milk and pudding mix for 2 minutes. Let stand for 2 minutes or until soft-set. Stir in 1 cup whipped topping. Fold in the remaining whipped topping; stir in extract.

4. Unroll cake; spread with filling to within 1 in. of edges. Arrange kiwi and strawberries over filling.

Sprinkle with ⅓ cup coconut. Roll up again. Refrigerate cake for 1-2 hours.

5. Toast the remaining coconut. In a small bowl, whisk spreadable fruit and water until smooth. Drizzle over cake. Sprinkle with toasted coconut. Cut into slices. Store in the refrigerator.

APRICOT-RASPBERRY ANGEL TORTE

Fresh raspberries lend a from-scratch touch to this gorgeous torte that is given a boost by canned pie filling.

—**SALLY SIBTHORPE** SHELBY TOWNSHIP, MI

PREP: 20 MIN. • **BAKE:** 35 MIN. + COOLING • **MAKES:** 12 SERVINGS

1 package (16 ounces) angel food cake mix
2 packages (one 8 ounces, one 3 ounces) cream cheese, softened
⅓ cup sugar
1¼ teaspoons almond extract
1 carton (8 ounces) frozen whipped topping, thawed
1 can (21 ounces) apricot or peach pie filling
1½ cups fresh raspberries
1 cup sliced almonds
Fresh mint leaves

1. Prepare and bake the cake according to package directions, using an ungreased 10-in. tube pan. Immediately invert pan; cool completely, about 1 hour. Run a knife around side and center tube of pan. Remove cake from pan.

2. In a large bowl, beat the cream cheese, sugar and extract until light and fluffy; fold in whipped topping.

3. Split the cake into three horizontal layers. Place bottom layer on a serving plate; spread with a third of the cream cheese mixture. Top with a third of the pie filling, raspberries and almonds. Repeat the layers twice. Garnish with the mint. Store in the refrigerator.

CHOCOLATE-CHERRY ANGEL CAKE

Here's a cake that will catch the eye of all your guests. It's beautiful and is ideal for parties or holidays.
If you love chocolate and cherries together, you'll love this cake!

—BARBARA WHEELER ROYAL OAK, MI

PREP: 20 MIN. • **BAKE:** 35 MIN. + COOLING • **MAKES:** 16 SERVINGS

- 1 package (16 ounces) angel food cake mix
- ½ cup finely chopped maraschino cherries
- 1 cup semisweet chocolate chips
- 1 tablespoon maraschino cherry juice
- 2 teaspoons strong brewed coffee
- 1 container (8 ounces) sour cream
- ½ teaspoon vanilla extract
- 1 container (8 ounces) frozen whipped topping, thawed
  Chopped walnuts, grated chocolate and additional maraschino cherries

1. Prepare the cake mix batter according to package directions; fold in chopped cherries. Gently spoon into an ungreased 10-in. tube pan. Cut through batter with a knife to remove air pockets.

2. Bake on the lowest oven rack at 350° for 45-55 minutes or until lightly browned and entire top appears dry. Immediately invert pan; cool completely, about 1 hour. Run a knife around side and center tube of pan. Cut cake horizontally into three layers.

3. For filling, in a small heavy saucepan, cook and stir the chocolate chips, cherry juice and coffee over medium-low heat until chocolate is melted. Remove from the heat; stir in sour cream and extract.

4. To assemble, place one cake layer on a serving plate; spread with one half of the filling. Repeat the layers. Top with remaining cake layer. Spread the whipped topping over top and sides of the cake. Garnish with the walnuts, chocolate and cherries. Store in the refrigerator.

FAST FIX APPLE-SPICE ANGEL FOOD CAKE

Angel food is a delectable dessert choice when you're watching your intake of fat and calories.
Apple pie spice and toasted nuts add festive fall flavor.

—JOAN BUEHNERKEMPER TEUTOPOLIS, IL

PREP: 10 MIN. • **BAKE:** 35 MIN. + COOLING • **MAKES:** 16 SERVINGS

- 1 package (16 ounces) angel food cake mix
- 1 cup water
- ⅔ cup unsweetened applesauce
- ½ cup finely chopped pecans, toasted
- 1 teaspoon apple pie spice
  Reduced-fat whipped topping and/or apple slices, optional

1. In a large bowl, combine cake mix and water. Beat on low speed for 30 seconds. Beat on medium speed for 1 minute. Fold in the applesauce, pecans and pie spice.

2. Gently spoon batter into an ungreased 10-in. tube pan. Cut through batter with a knife to remove air pockets. Bake on the lowest oven rack at 350° for 35-45 minutes or until lightly browned and entire top appears dry. Immediately invert pan; cool completely, about 1 hour.

3. Run a knife around side and center tube of pan. Remove cake to a serving plate. Garnish with whipped topping and/or apple slices if desired.

LUSCIOUS LEMON ANGEL ROLL

I came across this recipe while preparing for a party and was thrilled with how easy it was to make. My guests were impressed that I could use a few simple ingredients to create such a stylish dessert.

—PAMELA WRIGHT ST. HELENS, OR

PREP: 25 MIN. • **BAKE:** 30 MIN. + CHILLING • **MAKES:** 12 SERVINGS

- 1 **package (16 ounces) angel food cake mix**
- ¾ **cup confectioners' sugar, divided**
- 1 **package (8 ounces) cream cheese, softened**
- 1 **tablespoon lemon juice**
- 2 **teaspoons grated lemon peel**
- 6 **to 8 drops yellow food coloring, optional**
- 1 **carton (8 ounces) frozen whipped topping, thawed, divided**
- 1 **jar (11¾ ounces) strawberry ice cream topping, divided**
  Additional confectioners' sugar
- 12 **fresh strawberries**

1. Line a greased 15x10x1-in. baking pan with parchment paper; set aside. Prepare the cake batter according to the package directions. Spread evenly in the prepared pan.

2. Bake at 350° for 30-35 minutes or until cake springs back when lightly touched (cake rises above edges of pan). Cool for 5 minutes.

3. Sprinkle 2 tablespoons of the confectioners' sugar over a kitchen towel. Invert cake onto towel and gently peel off the parchment paper. Sprinkle with 2 tablespoons confectioners' sugar. Roll up cake in the towel jelly-roll style, starting with a short side. Cool completely on a wire rack.

4. In a small bowl, beat cream cheese, lemon juice and peel, food coloring if desired and remaining confectioners' sugar until smooth. Fold in 1 cup whipped topping.

5. Unroll cake. Spread ⅓ cup strawberry topping to within 1 in. of edges. Spread the cream cheese mixture over topping. Roll up again. Place seam side down on a serving platter. Cover and chill for 1 hour.

6. Dust with additional confectioners' sugar. Cut into slices; garnish with the fresh strawberries and remaining strawberry topping and whipped topping. Store in the refrigerator.

{6}

Bundt Cakes

155

Fluted Tiramisu Cake

161

Triple Chocolate Cake

168

Choco-Scotch Marble Cake

CINNAMON NUT CAKE

I use this easy-to-assemble treat for brunch or dessert. Top with a dollop of whipped cream and you're ready to enjoy.
—**MARGARET WILSON** SUN CITY, CA

PREP: 20 MIN. • **BAKE:** 35 MIN. • **MAKES:** 12-14 SERVINGS

1 **package yellow cake mix (regular size)**
3 **eggs**

1⅓ **cups water**
¼ **cup canola oil**
1¼ **cups finely chopped walnuts**

7½ **teaspoons sugar**
4½ **teaspoons ground cinnamon**

1. In a large bowl, combine cake mix, eggs, water and oil; beat on low speed 30 seconds. Beat on medium speed for 2 minutes. Mix walnuts, sugar and cinnamon.
2. Sprinkle a third of the nut mixture into a greased 10-in. fluted tube pan. Top with half of the batter and another third of the nut mixture. Repeat layers.
3. Bake at 350° for 35-40 minutes or until a toothpick inserted near the center comes out clean. Cool for 10 minutes before removing from the pan to a wire rack to cool completely.

PEPPERMINT RIBBON CAKE

With its pretty pink layer and fabulous mint flavor, this is a great holiday dessert. Because I work full-time, I like the fact that it starts with a convenient cake mix.
—**LISA VARNER** EL PASO, TX

PREP: 20 MIN. • **BAKE:** 35 MIN. + COOLING • **MAKES:** 12 SERVINGS

1 **package white cake mix (regular size)**
½ **teaspoon peppermint extract**
½ **teaspoon red food coloring**
½ **cup plus 2 tablespoons crushed peppermint candies, divided**
1 **cup confectioners' sugar**
1 **tablespoon 2% milk**

1. Prepare cake batter according to package directions. Transfer 1 cup to a small bowl; stir in the extract, food coloring and ½ cup crushed candies.
2. Spoon 2 cups of the remaining batter into a greased and floured 10-in. fluted tube pan. Carefully top with peppermint batter; do not swirl. Top with remaining plain batter.

3. Bake at 350° for 35-45 minutes or until a toothpick inserted near the center comes out clean. Cool for 10 minutes before removing from the pan to a wire rack to cool completely.
4. Combine the confectioners' sugar and milk; drizzle over the cake. Sprinkle with remaining crushed candies.

TRIPLE-CHOCOLATE CAKE WITH RASPBERRY SAUCE

Chocolate lovers, brace yourselves. This cocoa creation and its saucy accompaniment make a heavenly combination.

—JENNY STANIEC OAK GROVE, MN

PREP: 20 MIN. • **BAKE:** 1 HOUR + COOLING • **MAKES:** 12 SERVINGS (2⅔ CUPS SAUCE)

- 1 **package chocolate cake mix (regular size)**
- 1 **package (3.4 ounces) instant vanilla pudding mix**
- 1 **package (3.4 ounces) instant chocolate pudding mix**
- 4 **eggs**
- 1½ **cups water**
- ½ **cup canola oil**
- 1 **cup (6 ounces) semisweet chocolate chips**

RASPBERRY SAUCE
- 1 **cup water**
- 2 **packages (10 ounces each) frozen sweetened raspberries, thawed**
- 1 **tablespoon sugar**
- 3 **tablespoons cornstarch**
- 2 **tablespoons lemon juice**
  Confectioners' sugar

1. Preheat oven to 325°. In a large bowl, combine the cake mix, pudding mixes, eggs, water and oil; beat on low speed 30 seconds. Beat on medium 2 minutes. Fold in the chocolate chips. Pour into a well-greased 10-in. fluted tube pan.

2. Bake 60-65 minutes or until a toothpick inserted near center comes out clean. Cool 10 minutes before removing from pan to a wire rack to cool completely.

3. Meanwhile, place water, raspberries and sugar in a blender; cover and process until well blended. In a small saucepan, combine cornstarch and lemon juice; stir in raspberry puree. Bring to a boil. Cook and stir 2 minutes or until thickened. Refrigerate until serving.

4. Dust cake with confectioners' sugar. Serve with sauce.

FLUTED TIRAMISU CAKE

Melted coffee ice cream adds decadent depth of flavor to a white cake mix.
A simple yet impressive dessert, this cake will rise above your highest expectations.

—CAROL GILLESPIE CHAMBERSBURG, PA

PREP: 20 MIN. ● **BAKE:** 35 MIN. + COOLING ● **MAKES:** 12 SERVINGS

1 **package white cake mix (regular size)**
2 **cups coffee ice cream, melted**
3 **eggs**
1 **tablespoon water**
1 **teaspoon instant coffee granules**
1 **can (12 ounces) whipped vanilla frosting**
½ **teaspoon ground cinnamon**
1 **tablespoon cinnamon-sugar**

1. In a large bowl, beat the cake mix, ice cream and eggs at low speed for 30 seconds. Beat on medium for 2 minutes. Pour into a greased and floured 10-in. fluted tube pan.

2. Bake at 350° for 35-40 minutes or until a toothpick inserted near the center comes out clean. Cool for 10 minutes before removing from the pan to a wire rack to cool completely.

3. Place the water and coffee granules in a large bowl; stir until dissolved. Add the frosting and cinnamon; beat until smooth. Frost the cake. Sprinkle with the cinnamon-sugar.

PUMPKIN SPICE CAKE WITH MAPLE GLAZE

Serve up some fun with my delicious cake that's yummy any time of the year, but especially nice during the holiday season. The traditional pumpkin and spices plus the delectable maple glaze give it a real homemade taste.
—BARBARA ELLIOTT TYLER, TX

PREP: 20 MIN. • **BAKE:** 45 MIN. + COOLING • **MAKES:** 12 SERVINGS

1 **package yellow cake mix (regular size)**
1 **can (15 ounces) solid-pack pumpkin**
4 **eggs**
½ **cup canola oil**
⅓ **cup sugar**
2 **tablespoons ground cinnamon**
1 **teaspoon ground ginger**
1 **teaspoon ground allspice**
1 **teaspoon ground nutmeg**
¼ **teaspoon ground cloves**
GLAZE
2 **cups confectioners' sugar**
¼ **cup 2% milk**
2 **tablespoons maple syrup**
½ **teaspoon maple flavoring**
½ **cup chopped pecans, toasted**

1. Place the first 10 ingredients in a large bowl; beat on low speed for 30 seconds. Beat on medium for 2 minutes. Pour into a greased and floured 10-in. fluted tube pan.
2. Bake at 350° for 45-50 minutes or until a toothpick inserted near the center comes out clean. Cool for 10 minutes before removing from the pan to a wire rack to cool completely.
3. Whisk confectioners' sugar, milk, syrup and maple flavoring until smooth. Drizzle over cake and sprinkle with pecans.

ORANGE-LEMON CAKE

You'll be delighted with the double dose of orange flavor in my dessert. The orange-lemon cake is topped with a simple orange glaze—yum!

—ANN ROBINSON BLOOMINGTON, IN

PREP: 15 MIN.
BAKE: 35 MIN. + COOLING
MAKES: 12 SERVINGS

- 1 **package lemon cake mix (regular size)**
- 1 **package (3 ounces) orange gelatin**
- ⅔ **cup water**
- ⅔ **cup canola oil**
- 4 **eggs**

ICING

- 1 **cup confectioners' sugar**
- 3 **to 4 teaspoons orange juice**

1. In a large bowl, combine the cake mix, gelatin, water, oil and eggs; beat on low speed for 30 seconds. Beat on medium for 2 minutes. Pour into a greased and floured 10-in. fluted tube pan.

2. Bake at 350° for 35-40 minutes or until a toothpick inserted near the center comes out clean. Cool for 10 minutes before removing from the pan to a wire rack to cool completely.

3. Combine confectioners' sugar and enough orange juice to reach desired consistency. Drizzle over the cake.

FAST FIX ▶ PEAR BUNDT CAKE

Five kitchen staples are all that's needed to fix this light and lovely dessert.
Tiny bits of pear provide sweetness to the moist slices.
—**VERONICA ROSS** COLUMBIA HEIGHTS, MN

PREP: 15 MIN. • **BAKE:** 50 MIN. • **MAKES:** 16 SERVINGS

- 1 **can (15 ounces) reduced-sugar sliced pears**
- 1 **package white cake mix (regular size)**
- 2 **egg whites**
- 1 **egg**
- 2 **teaspoons confectioners' sugar**

1. Drain pears, reserving the syrup; chop pears. Place pears and syrup in a large bowl; add the cake mix, egg whites and egg. Beat on low speed for 30 seconds. Beat on high for 4 minutes.
2. Coat a 10-in. fluted tube pan with cooking spray and dust with flour. Add batter.

3. Bake at 350° for 50-55 minutes or until a toothpick inserted near the center comes out clean. Cool for 10 minutes before removing from pan to a wire rack to cool completely. Dust with the confectioners' sugar.

ORANGE CHOCOLATE CAKE

One of the best cooks in my ladies' Bible class at church shared her cake recipe with me.
The orange and chocolate combination is delicious. One of my hobbies is collecting recipes,
especially those for desserts, which suits my chocolate-loving husband just fine!
—**LINDA HARRIS** WICHITA, KS

PREP: 20 MIN. • **BAKE:** 1 HOUR + COOLING • **MAKES:** 16-20 SERVINGS

- 1 **package orange cake mix (regular size)**
- 5 **eggs**
- 1 **cup orange juice or water**
- 1 **package (3.4 ounces) instant vanilla pudding mix**
- 1 **teaspoon orange extract, optional**
- ½ **cup semisweet chocolate chips**
- ½ **cup chopped walnuts or pecans**
- ¾ **cup chocolate syrup**

1. In a large bowl, beat the cake mix, eggs, juice, pudding mix and extract if desired until well blended and smooth. Sprinkle chocolate chips and nuts into a greased and floured 10-in. fluted tube pan. Pour two-thirds of batter into pan. Combine the chocolate syrup with remaining batter; pour into pan.
2. Bake at 350° for 1 hour or until a toothpick inserted near the center comes out clean. Cool for 10 minutes before inverting onto wire rack.

FAST FIX ▸ EGGNOG TUBE CAKE

My kids have declared this dessert one of their favorites. They love its festive eggnog flavor.

—MARY ELLEN SEVERANCE BIGGS, CA

PREP: 15 MIN.
BAKE: 40 MIN. + COOLING
MAKES: 12 SERVINGS

- 1 **package white cake mix (regular size)**
- 1 **package (3.9 ounces) instant vanilla pudding mix**
- 4 **eggs**
- 1 **cup eggnog**
- ¼ **cup canola oil**
- 2 **teaspoons rum extract**
- 1½ **teaspoons ground nutmeg**

GLAZE

- 1 **cup confectioners' sugar**
- ¼ **teaspoon rum extract**
- 3 **to 4 teaspoons eggnog**

1. In a large bowl, combine the cake mix, pudding mix, eggs, eggnog, oil, extract and nutmeg; beat on low speed for 30 seconds. Beat on medium for 2 minutes. Pour into a well-greased 10-in. fluted tube pan.

2. Bake at 350° for 38-41 minutes or until a toothpick inserted near the center comes out clean. Cool on a wire rack for 10 minutes before removing from pan to a wire rack to cool completely.

3. In a small bowl, combine the confectioners' sugar, extract and enough eggnog to reach a drizzling consistency. Drizzle over cooled cake.

NOTE *This recipe was tested with commercially prepared eggnog.*

FAST FIX ▸ TRIPLE CHOCOLATE CAKE

Sour cream adds richness to this treat and the chips sprinkle in some fun. The whole family will love the chocolaty results and your pocketbook will love that it doesn't cost much to make!
—**MELISSA JUST** MINNEAPOLIS, MN

PREP: 15 MIN. • **BAKE:** 45 MIN. + COOLING • **MAKES:** 12 SERVINGS

1 **package white cake mix (regular size)**
⅓ **cup sugar**
4 **eggs**
1 **cup (8 oz.) sour cream**
⅔ **cup canola oil**
2 **tablespoons baking cocoa**
½ **cup miniature semisweet chocolate chips**
1 **cup chocolate frosting**
2 **tablespoons 2% milk**

1. In a large bowl, combine the cake mix, sugar, eggs, sour cream and oil. Beat on low for 1 minute; beat on medium for 2 minutes. Pour half of the batter into a large bowl. Stir in cocoa until blended. Fold chocolate chips into white cake batter.

2. Alternately spoon batters into a greased and floured 10-in. fluted tube pan.

3. Bake at 350° for 45-50 minutes or until a toothpick inserted near the center comes out clean. Cool for 15 minutes before removing from pan to a wire rack to cool completely.

4. In a small bowl, combine the frosting and milk. Spoon over top of cooled cake.

FAST FIX ► CHOCOLATE CHIP CAKE

Here's a scrumptious cake that's easy to transport and fun to serve at potlucks because everyone likes it!

—ABIGAIL CRAWFORD LAKE BUTLER, FL

PREP: 15 MIN. • **BAKE:** 55 MIN. + COOLING • **MAKES:** 12 SERVINGS

- 1 **package yellow cake mix (regular size)**
- 1 **package (3.4 ounces) instant vanilla pudding mix**
- 1 **cup 2% milk**
- 1 **cup canola oil**
- 4 **eggs**
- 1 **cup miniature semisweet chocolate chips**
- 5 **tablespoons grated German sweet chocolate, divided**
- 2 **tablespoons confectioners' sugar**

1. In a large bowl, combine the cake and pudding mixes, milk, oil and eggs. Beat on low speed for 30 seconds. Beat on medium for 2 minutes. Stir in chocolate chips and 3 tablespoons grated chocolate. Pour into a greased and floured 10-in. fluted tube pan.

2. Bake at 350° for 55-65 minutes or until a toothpick inserted near the center comes out clean. Cool for 10 minutes: remove from pan to a wire rack to cool completely.

3. Combine confectioners' sugar and remaining grated chocolate; sprinkle over cake.

PISTACHIO CAKE WITH WALNUTS

It didn't take long for this cake from the 1970s to become the favorite birthday cake of my husband, Joe.

—PATTY LANOUE STEARNS TRAVERSE CITY, MI

PREP: 20 MIN. • **BAKE:** 40 MIN + COOLING • **MAKES:** 12 SERVINGS

- 1 **package white cake mix (regular size)**
- 1 **package (3.4 ounces) instant pistachio pudding mix**
- 3 **eggs**
- 1 **cup club soda**
- ¾ **cup canola oil**
- 1 **cup chopped walnuts**
- **FROSTING**
- 1 **package (3.4 ounces) instant pistachio pudding mix**
- 1 **cup 2% milk**
- 1 **carton (8 ounces) frozen whipped topping, thawed**

1. Preheat oven to 350°. Grease and flour a 10-in. fluted tube pan.

2. In a large bowl, combine first five ingredients; beat on low speed 30 seconds. Beat on medium 2 minutes. Fold in the walnuts. Transfer to prepared pan.

3. Bake 40-45 minutes or until a toothpick inserted in center comes out clean. Cool in pan 10 minutes before removing to a wire rack to cool completely.

4. For frosting, in a large bowl, combine pudding mix and milk; beat on low speed 1 minute. Fold in whipped topping. Spread over cake. Store in the refrigerator.

FAST FIX ▸ CHOCOLATE BUNDT CAKE

Chocolate lovers will delight in this moist, rich cake that uses handy mixes and canned frosting. I only make this dessert if I'm taking it somewhere. I don't want it sitting in my kitchen, where I might be tempted to eat it all!

—NANCY BAKER BOONVILLE, MO

PREP: 15 MIN. • **BAKE:** 1 HOUR + COOLING • **MAKES:** 12-14 SERVINGS

- **1 package yellow cake mix (regular size)**
- **1 package (3.4 ounces) instant vanilla pudding mix**
- **1 cup (8 ounces) sour cream**
- **3 eggs**
- **½ cup canola oil**
- **½ cup water**
- **4 ounces German sweet chocolate, grated**
- **1 cup (6 ounces) semisweet chocolate chips**

- **½ cup chopped pecans**
- **½ cup chocolate frosting, melted**
- **Pecan halves**

1. Preheat oven to 350°. In a large bowl, combine the cake and pudding mixes, sour cream, eggs, oil and water; beat on low speed 30 seconds. Beat on medium 2 minutes. Fold in the grated chocolate, chocolate chips and pecans. Transfer to a greased and floured 10-in. fluted tube pan.

2. Bake 60-65 minutes or until a toothpick inserted near center comes out clean. Cool 10 minutes before removing from pan to a wire rack. Drizzle with frosting; garnish with pecan halves.

FAST FIX → GLAZED FLUTED LEMON CAKE

My husband says this is the best lemon cake he's ever eaten, which is good for me since it's so easy to do.
—BRENDA DAUGHERTY LAKE CITY, FL

PREP: 15 MIN. ● **BAKE:** 40 MIN. + COOLING ● **MAKES:** 12-16 SERVINGS

1 **package yellow cake mix (regular size)**
1 **package (3 ounces) lemon gelatin**
4 **eggs**
⅔ **cup water**
⅔ **cup canola oil**
GLAZE
1 **cup confectioners' sugar**

3 **tablespoons lemon juice**
1 **teaspoon grated lemon peel**

1. In a large bowl, combine the cake mix, gelatin, eggs, water and oil. Beat on low speed for 1 minute. Beat on medium for 2 minutes. Pour into a greased and floured 10-in. fluted tube pan.

2. Bake at 350° for 38-42 minutes or until a toothpick inserted near the center comes out clean. Cool for 10 minutes before removing from pan to a wire rack.
3. Combine glaze ingredients; drizzle over warm cake. Cool completely before cutting.

POPPY SEED CITRUS CAKE

My youngest daughter loves anything with lemon, and this is the cake she most desires.
It's refreshing and easy to pack for picnics.
—CHAROLETTE WESTFALL HOUSTON, TX

PREP: 15 MIN. • **BAKE:** 40 MIN. + COOLING • **MAKES:** 12 SERVINGS

- 1 **package lemon cake mix (regular size)**
- 3 **eggs**
- 1⅓ **cups orange juice**
- ½ **cup canola oil**
- 1 **to 2 tablespoons poppy seeds**
- 1 **teaspoon grated lemon peel**
- 1 **teaspoon grated orange peel**

GLAZE
- 2 **cups confectioners' sugar**
- 3 **to 4 tablespoons orange juice**
- ½ **teaspoon grated lemon peel**
- ½ **teaspoon grated orange peel**

1. In a large bowl, combine cake mix, eggs, orange juice and oil; beat on low speed for 30 seconds. Beat on medium for 2 minutes. Fold in poppy seeds and lemon and orange peel. Pour into a well-greased and floured 10-in. fluted tube pan.

2. Bake at 350° for 40-45 minutes or until a toothpick inserted near the center comes out clean. Cool for 10 minutes before removing from the pan to a wire rack to cool completely.

3. In a small bowl, combine the confectioners' sugar and orange juice until smooth. Drizzle over warm cake. Sprinkle with lemon and orange peel.

BANANA CHIP CAKE

Here's my version of Ben & Jerry's Chunky Monkey Ice Cream (my favorite!) in a cake.
The hardest part is waiting for it to cool.
—BARBARA PRYOR MILFORD, MA

PREP: 25 MIN. • **BAKE:** 40 MIN. + COOLING • **MAKES:** 16 SERVINGS

- 1 **package yellow cake mix (regular size)**
- 1¼ **cups water**
- 3 **eggs**
- ½ **cup unsweetened applesauce**
- 2 **medium bananas, mashed**
- 1 **cup miniature semisweet chocolate chips**
- ½ **cup chopped walnuts**

1. Coat a 10-in. fluted tube pan with cooking spray and sprinkled with flour; set aside.

2. In a large bowl, combine cake mix, water, eggs and applesauce; beat on low speed for 30 seconds. Beat on medium for 2 minutes. Stir in bananas, chips and nuts. Transfer to a prepared pan.

3. Bake at 350° for 40-50 minutes or until a toothpick inserted near the center comes out clean. Cool for 10 minutes before removing from the pan to a wire rack to cool completely.

CHOCO-SCOTCH MARBLE CAKE

This recipe was given to me many years ago by a friend. Teaming chocolate with butterscotch for a marble cake makes it more flavorful and colorful than the usual chocolate-vanilla combination. This rich family favorite is very moist and keeps well.

—PAM GIAMMATTEI VALATIE, NY

PREP: 15 MIN. • **BAKE:** 40 MIN. + COOLING • **MAKES:** 12 SERVINGS

- 1 **package yellow cake mix (regular size)**
- 1 **package (3.4 ounces) instant butterscotch pudding mix**
- 4 **eggs**
- 1 **cup (8 ounces) sour cream**
- ⅓ **cup canola oil**
- ½ **cup butterscotch chips**
- 1 **ounce unsweetened chocolate, melted**

FROSTING

- 1½ **cups butterscotch chips, melted**
- 1 **ounce unsweetened chocolate, melted**
- 5 **to 6 tablespoons half-and-half cream**
- 2 **tablespoons finely chopped pecans**

1. In a large bowl, combine the cake mix, pudding mix, eggs, sour cream and oil; beat on low speed for 30 seconds. Beat on medium for 2 minutes. Divide batter in half; stir butterscotch chips into half and chocolate into the other half.

2. Spoon half of the butterscotch batter in a greased and floured 10-in. fluted tube pan; top with half of the chocolate batter. Repeat layers. Cut through batter with a knife to swirl.

3. Bake at 350° for 40-45 minutes or until a toothpick inserted near the center comes out clean. Cool for 10 minutes before removing from pan to a wire rack to cool completely.

4. For frosting, in a small bowl, combine butterscotch chips and chocolate. Beat in enough cream until the frosting is smooth and reaches desired spreading consistency. Spread over top of cake. Sprinkle with pecans.

{7}

Cookies & Bars

174

Lemon Crumb Bars

182

Apple Oatmeal Cookies

200

Blueberry Crumb Bars

FAST FIX ▸ BUTTERSCOTCH-TOFFEE CHEESECAKE BARS

I'd been making my lemon cheesecake bar recipe for years and wanted a new flavor combo. Using the original bar as a starting point, I tried a butterscotch and toffee version. The results were sweetly satisfying!

—PAMELA SHANK PARKERSBURG, WV

PREP: 10 MIN. • **BAKE:** 30 MIN. + CHILLING • **MAKES:** 2 DOZEN

- 1 **package yellow cake mix (regular size)**
- 1 **package (3.4 ounces) instant butterscotch pudding mix**
- ⅓ **cup canola oil**
- 2 **eggs**
- 1 **package (8 ounces) cream cheese, softened**
- ⅓ **cup sugar**
- 1 **cup brickle toffee bits, divided**
- ½ **cup butterscotch chips**

1. In a large bowl, combine the cake mix, pudding mix, oil and 1 egg until crumbly. Set aside 1 cup for topping. Press the remaining mixture into an ungreased 13x9-in. baking pan. Bake at 350° for 10 minutes. Cool completely on a wire rack.

2. In a small bowl, beat cream cheese and sugar until smooth. Add the remaining egg; beat on low speed just until combined. Fold in ½ cup toffee bits. Spread over crust. Sprinkle with reserved crumb mixture. Bake for 15-20 minutes or until filling is set.

3. Sprinkle with butterscotch chips and remaining toffee bits. Return to oven for 1 minute. Cool on a wire rack for 1 hour. Chill for at least 2 hours. Cut into bars. Store in the refrigerator.

APRICOT COCONUT BARS

I created this recipe one winter's day and shared it with a friend. I've had many favorable comments from those who've sampled it since. Great apricot flavor and sprinkling of coconut make these bars special!

—**BARBARA ROHLF** SPIRIT LAKE, IA

PREP: 25 MIN. • **BAKE:** 25 MIN. + COOLING • **MAKES:** 2 DOZEN

- 1 **package (16 ounces) pound cake mix**
- 4 **eggs**
- ½ **cup butter, melted**
- 2 **teaspoons vanilla extract, divided**
- 1 **cup chopped dried apricots**
- 1 **package (8 ounces) cream cheese, softened**
- 2 **cups confectioners' sugar**
- ½ **cup apricot preserves**

- ¾ **cup flaked coconut**
- ¾ **cup sliced almonds**

1. In a large bowl, combine cake mix, 2 eggs, butter and 1 teaspoon vanilla; beat until well blended. Fold in dried apricots. Spread into a greased 15x10x1-in. baking pan; set aside.

2. In another bowl, beat cream cheese, confectioners' sugar, preserves and remaining vanilla. Add remaining eggs; beat on low speed just until combined. Gently spread over cake batter. Sprinkle with coconut and almonds.

3. Bake at 350° for 25-30 minutes or until golden brown. Cool on a wire rack. Cut into bars. Store in the refrigerator.

MINT-TOPPED CHOCOLATE COOKIES

My neighbor shared her cookie recipe that combines two of my favorite flavors—mint and chocolate!

—JENNIFER BURNS MCMURRAY, PA

PREP: 20 MIN. • **BAKE:** 10 MIN./BATCH + COOLING • **MAKES:** 40 COOKIES

1 package devil's food cake mix
   (regular size)
½ cup shortening
2 eggs
1 tablespoon water
   Confectioners' sugar
40 chocolate-covered thin mints

1. In a large bowl, combine the cake mix, shortening, eggs and water. Shape into 1-in. balls; roll in confectioners' sugar. Place 2 in. apart on ungreased baking sheets.
2. Bake at 350° for 8-10 minutes or until slightly firm to the touch. Place a mint on each cookie; remove to wire racks to cool.
NOTE *These cookies were tested with Necco Thin Mints. They can be found at Walgreens stores.*

FAST FIX ▸ CHOCOLATE PEANUT BUTTER COOKIES

It's a snap to make a batch of tasty cookies using this recipe. My husband and son gobble them up.

—MARY PULYER PORT ST. LUCIE, FL

PREP: 10 MIN. • **BAKE:** 10 MIN./BATCH • **MAKES:** 4 DOZEN

1 package devil's food cake mix
   (regular size)
2 eggs
⅓ cup canola oil
1 package (10 ounces) peanut
   butter chips

1. In a bowl, beat cake mix, eggs and oil (batter will be very stiff). Stir in chips.
2. Roll into 1-in. balls. Place on lightly greased baking sheets; flatten slightly.

3. Bake at 350° for 10 minutes or until a slight indentation remains when lightly touched. Cool for 2 minutes before removing to a wire rack.

FAST FIX ▶ LEMON CRUMB BARS

I'm always looking for a great new cookie or bar to try, but I often return this tried-and-true recipe.
My husband loves the combination of sweet and salty!

—**ANNA MILLER** QUAKER CITY, OH

PREP: 15 MIN. • **BAKE:** 40 MIN. + COOLING • **MAKES:** 2 DOZEN

---

1 **package lemon cake mix (regular size)**
½ **cup cold butter, cubed**
1 **egg**
2 **cups crushed saltines (about 60 crackers)**
3 **egg yolks**
1 **can (14 ounces) sweetened condensed milk**
½ **cup lemon juice**

1. In a large bowl, beat the cake mix, butter and egg until crumbly. Stir in cracker crumbs; set aside 2 cups for topping.

2. Press remaining mixture into a 13x9-in. baking dish coated with cooking spray. Bake at 350° for 18-20 minutes or until edges are lightly browned.

3. In a small bowl, beat the egg yolks, milk and lemon juice. Pour over crust; sprinkle with reserved topping. Bake 20-25 minutes longer or until edges are lightly browned. Cool on a wire rack. Cut into bars. Store in the refrigerator.

CHOCOLATE CHIP CREAM CHEESE BARS

Lower in fat and calories than you might ever guess, these delightful bars couldn't be easier to whip up. They boast a great chocolaty flavor and make a fun, quick dessert to bring to parties or serve to company!

—JENNIFER RAFFERTY MILFORD, OH

PREP: 20 MIN. • **BAKE:** 20 MIN. + COOLING • **MAKES:** 2 DOZEN

1 **package German chocolate cake mix (regular size)**
⅓ **cup canola oil**
1 **egg**
FILLING
1 **package (8 ounces) reduced-fat cream cheese**
⅓ **cup sugar**
1 **egg**
1 **cup miniature semisweet chocolate chips**

1. In a large bowl, combine the cake mix, oil and egg. Set aside 1 cup for topping. Press the remaining crumb mixture into a 13x9-in. baking pan coated with cooking spray. Bake at 350° for 10-12 minutes or until set.

2. For filling, in a large bowl, beat cream cheese and sugar until smooth. Add the egg; beat well. Spread over crust. Sprinkle with chocolate chips and reserved crumb mixture.

3. Bake for 18-20 minutes or until set. Cool on a wire rack. Cut into bars. Store in the refrigerator.

CHOCOLATE CAKE COOKIES

I love these soft, chewy cookies. They take just a few minutes to make and are easy enough for kids to help out.

—MONICA STOUT ANCHORAGE, AK

PREP: 30 MIN. • **BAKE:** 10 MIN./BATCH • **MAKES:** 7 DOZEN

- **1 package chocolate fudge cake mix (regular size)**
- **2 packages (3.9 ounces each) instant chocolate fudge pudding mix**
- **1½ cups mayonnaise**
- **2 cups (12 ounces) semisweet chocolate chips**
- **½ cup chopped walnuts**

1. In a large bowl, combine cake mix, pudding mixes and mayonnaise; mix well. Stir in chocolate chips and walnuts.

2. Shape by teaspoonfuls into balls; place 2 in. apart on greased baking sheets.

3. Bake at 350° for 9-10 minutes or until cookies puff and surface cracks slightly. Cool for 5 minutes before removing from pans to wire racks.

STRAWBERRY JAM BARS

I bake for a group of seniors every week, and this is one of the goodies they request most. I always keep the ingredients on hand for last-minute baking emergencies. Give these bars your own twist by replacing the strawberry jam with the fruit filling of your choice.

—KAREN MEAD PITTSBURGH, PA

PREP: 15 MIN. • **BAKE:** 30 MIN.
MAKES: 2 DOZEN

- ½ **cup butter, softened**
- ½ **cup packed brown sugar**
- 1 **egg**
- 1 **package white cake mix (regular size)**
- 1 **cup finely crushed cornflakes**
- 1 **cup strawberry jam**

1. In a large bowl, cream butter and brown sugar until smooth. Add egg; mix well. Gradually add dry cake mix and cornflakes. Set aside 1½ cups for topping. Press remaining dough into a greased 13x9-in. baking pan. Carefully spread jam over crust. Sprinkle with the reserved dough; gently press down.
2. Bake at 350° for 30 minutes or until golden brown. Cool completely on a wire rack. Cut into bars.

FAST FIX ▸ LEMON CRISP COOKIES

Here's a quick-to-fix treat that's perfect to make when you've forgotten a treat for a bake sale or potluck. These cake-based, lemony gems only take 10 minutes to whip together. The sunny yellow color, big citrus flavor and delightful crunch are sure to bring smiles.

—JULIA LIVINGSTON FROSTPROOF, FL

START TO FINISH: 30 MIN.
MAKES: ABOUT 4 DOZEN

- 1 **package lemon cake mix (regular size)**
- 1 **cup crisp rice cereal**
- ½ **cup butter, melted**
- 1 **egg, lightly beaten**
- 1 **teaspoon grated lemon peel**

1. In a large bowl, combine all the ingredients (dough will be crumbly). Shape into 1-in. balls. Place 2 in. apart on ungreased baking sheets.

2. Bake at 350° for 10-12 minutes or until set. Cool for 1 minute before removing from pan to a wire rack to cool completely.

BUTTER PECAN BISCOTTI

If you like to have a sweet to dunk in your coffee, this crisp biscotti is an ideal candidate for the job.

—TASTE OF HOME TEST KITCHEN

PREP: 25 MIN. • **BAKE:** 40 MIN. + COOLING • **MAKES:** ABOUT 2 DOZEN

- 1 **package butter pecan cake mix (regular size)**
- 1 **cup all-purpose flour**
- ½ **cup butter, melted**
- 2 **eggs**
- 3 **tablespoons maple syrup**
- 2½ **teaspoons instant coffee granules**
- 1 **teaspoon vanilla extract**
- 1 **cup white baking chips**
- 1 **cup confectioners' sugar**
- 2 **tablespoons brewed coffee**
- 1 **cup finely chopped pecans**

1. In a large bowl, beat the cake mix, flour, butter, eggs, syrup, coffee granules and vanilla until well blended (dough will be very thick). Fold in the chips. Divide dough in half.

2. On an ungreased baking sheet, shape each portion into a 12x2-in. rectangle. Bake at 350° for 30-35 minutes or until golden brown.

3. Place pans on wire racks. When cool enough to handle, transfer to a cutting board; cut diagonally with a serrated knife into ¾-in. slices. Place the slices cut side down on ungreased baking sheets.

4. Bake for 10-15 minutes or until firm. Remove to wire racks to cool completely.

5. In a small bowl, combine confectioners' sugar and coffee. Drizzle over biscotti; sprinkle with pecans. Let stand until set. Store in an airtight container.

MILLION DOLLAR PECAN BARS

Who wants to eat like a millionaire? Invest 15 minutes of your time, and enjoy a big payoff when you pull these rich bars of golden layered delight from the oven.

—LAURA DAVIS RUSK, TX

PREP: 15 MIN. • **BAKE:** 20 MIN. • **MAKES:** 2 DOZEN

- ¾ **cup butter, softened**
- ¾ **cup packed brown sugar**
- 2 **eggs**
- 2 **teaspoons vanilla extract**
- 1 **package butter pecan cake mix (regular size)**
- 2½ **cups quick-cooking oats**

FILLING

- 1 **can (14 ounces) sweetened condensed milk**
- 2 **cups milk chocolate chips**
- 1 **cup butterscotch chips**
- 1 **tablespoon butter**
- 1 **teaspoon vanilla extract**
- 1½ **cups chopped pecans**

1. In a large bowl, cream butter and brown sugar until light and fluffy. Add eggs, one at a time, beating well after each addition. Beat in vanilla. Add cake mix just until blended. Stir in oats. Press 3 cups onto the bottom of a greased 13x9-in. baking pan.

2. In a large microwave-safe bowl, combine milk and chips. Microwave, uncovered, on high for 2 minutes; stir. Cook 1-2½ minutes longer or until chips are melted, stirring every 30 seconds. Stir in butter and vanilla until butter is melted. Stir in pecans. Spread over crust. Crumble the remaining oat mixture; sprinkle over top.

3. Bake at 350° for 20-25 minutes or until topping is golden brown. Cool on a wire rack. Cut into bars.

GOOEY CHOCOLATE COOKIES

These soft and chewy cookies couldn't be easier to make.
Jazz them up with a chocolate kiss in the center, or substitute a different flavor of cake mix.

—ANGELA BAILEY SAN PIERRE, IN

PREP: 15 MIN. + CHILLING • **BAKE:** 10 MIN./BATCH • **MAKES:** 4½ DOZEN

- **1 package (8 ounces) cream cheese, softened**
- **½ cup butter, softened**
- **1 egg**
- **1 teaspoon vanilla extract**
- **1 package chocolate cake mix (regular size)**

1. In a large bowl, beat the cream cheese and butter until light and fluffy. Beat in egg and vanilla. Add cake mix and mix well (dough will be sticky). Cover and refrigerate for 2 hours.

2. Roll rounded tablespoonfuls of dough into balls. Place 2 in. apart on ungreased baking sheets.

3. Bake at 350° for 9-11 minutes or until tops are cracked. Cool for 2 minutes before removing from pans to wire racks.

APPLE OATMEAL COOKIES

I brought these yummy cookies to work and they were gone in seconds. They're a great snack, and addictive too!

—NICKI WOODS SPRINGFIELD, MO

PREP: 10 MIN.
BAKE: 15 MIN./BATCH
MAKES: ABOUT 5 DOZEN

- 1 **package yellow cake mix (regular size)**
- 1½ **cups quick-cooking oats**
- ½ **cup packed brown sugar**
- 2 **teaspoons ground cinnamon**
- 1 **egg**
- ¾ **cup unsweetened applesauce**
- 1 **cup finely chopped peeled apple**
- ½ **cup raisins**

1. In a large bowl, combine the cake mix, oats, brown sugar and cinnamon. In a small bowl, combine the egg, applesauce, apple and raisins. Stir into oat mixture and mix well.

2. Drop by heaping teaspoonfuls 2 in. apart onto baking sheets coated with cooking spray.

3. Bake at 350° for 12-14 minutes or until golden brown. Let stand for 2 minutes before removing to wire racks to cool.

BUTTERFINGER COOKIE BARS

My boys went through a phase where they loved Butterfingers. We made Butterfinger shakes, muffins and cookies, and experimented with different bars. This one was voted the best of the bunch. Make sure you have an extra candy bar on hand because it's hard to resist a nibble or two while you're chopping.
—BARBARA LEIGHTY SIMI VALLEY, CA

PREP: 20 MIN. • **BAKE:** 25 MIN. + COOLING • **MAKES:** 3 DOZEN

- 1 **package dark chocolate cake mix (regular size)**
- 1 **cup all-purpose flour**
- 1 **package (3.9 ounces) instant chocolate pudding mix**
- 1 **tablespoon baking cocoa**
- ½ **cup 2% milk**
- ⅓ **cup canola oil**
- ⅓ **cup butter, melted**
- 2 **eggs, divided**
- 6 **Butterfinger candy bars (2.1 ounces each), divided**
- 1½ **cups chunky peanut butter**
- 1 **teaspoon vanilla extract**
- 1½ **cups semisweet chocolate chips, divided**

1. Preheat oven to 350°. In a large bowl, combine cake mix, flour, pudding mix and cocoa. In another bowl, whisk milk, oil, butter and 1 egg until blended. Add to dry ingredients; stir just until moistened. Press half of the mixture into a greased 15x10x1-in. baking pan. Bake 10 minutes.
2. Meanwhile, chop two candy bars. Stir peanut butter, vanilla and remaining egg into remaining cake mix mixture. Fold in chopped bars and 1 cup chocolate chips.
3. Chop three additional candy bars; sprinkle over warm crust and press down gently. Cover with cake mix mixture; press down firmly with a metal spatula. Crush the remaining candy bar; sprinkle crushed bar and remaining chocolate chips over top.

4. Bake 25-30 minutes longer or until a toothpick inserted in the center comes out clean. Cool on a wire rack. Cut into bars. Store in an airtight container.

DEVIL'S FOOD COOKIES

Most people can't guess that these cookies are low in fat. You actually get more than two dozen of the treats from a cake mix plus four other common ingredients.

—MELANIE VAN DEN BRINK ROCK RAPIDS, IA

PREP: 15 MIN. • **BAKE:** 10 MIN./BATCH • **MAKES:** 28 COOKIES

- **1 package devil's food cake mix (regular size)**
- **2 eggs**
- **2 tablespoons butter, softened**
- **3 tablespoons water**
- **½ cup miniature semisweet chocolate chips**

1. Preheat oven to 350°. In a large bowl, combine cake mix, eggs, butter and water (batter will be thick). Fold in chocolate chips.

2. Drop by tablespoonfuls 2 in. apart onto baking sheets coated with cooking spray. Bake 10-13 minutes or until set and edges are lightly browned. Cool 2 minutes before removing to wire racks.

OLD-FASHIONED OAT-RAISIN COOKIES

I've been making these cookies for nearly 30 years. The flavor is delicious and they are always well-appreciated. This is an all-time favorite with my family.

—NANCY HORTON GREENBRIER, TN

PREP: 10 MIN. • **BAKE:** 10 MIN./BATCH • **MAKES:** 7 DOZEN

- **¾ cup canola oil**
- **¼ cup packed brown sugar**
- **2 eggs**
- **½ cup 2% milk**
- **1 package spice cake mix (regular size)**
- **2 cups old-fashioned oats**
- **2½ cups raisins**
- **1 cup chopped pecans**

1. In a large bowl, beat oil and brown sugar until blended. Beat in eggs, then milk. Combine cake mix and oats; gradually add to brown sugar mixture and mix well. Fold in raisins and pecans.

2. Drop by tablespoonfuls 2 in. apart onto greased baking sheets.

3. Bake at 350° for 10-12 minutes or until golden brown. Cool for 1 minute before removing to wire racks.

CHUBBY BUNNIES

This soft cookie bakes up in minutes. And kids will enjoy adding the simple decorations.
Sounds like the perfect Easter treat.

—TASTE OF HOME TEST KITCHEN

PREP: 20 MIN. • **BAKE:** 5 MIN./BATCH + COOLING • **MAKES:** 16 BUNNIES

- 1 **package yellow cake mix (regular size)**
- 2 **eggs**
- ½ **cup water**
- 15 **drops red food coloring**
- 16 **red gumdrops**
- 32 **miniature semisweet chocolate chips**

1. In a large bowl, combine the cake mix, eggs and water; beat on low speed for 30 seconds. Beat on medium for 2 minutes. Reserve 1 cup batter. To remaining batter, stir in food coloring. Cut a ¼-in. hole at the corner of two food-safe plastic bags; fill one with pink batter and one with plain batter.

2. Using pink batter, pipe a 4x2-in. oval ring onto a greased baking sheet for bunny face. Pipe two ovals for ears. Using plain batter, pipe centers for ears and cheeks for face. Pipe additional pink batter to completely fill ears and face. Repeat with remaining batters.

3. Trim off bottom ends of gumdrops; use rounded tops for noses. Add chocolate chips for the eyes.

4. Bake at 375° for 4-6 minutes or until set. Cool for 1 minute before removing to wire racks to cool. Store in an airtight container.

SWEET & SALTY CRANBERRY BARS

The sweet and salty flavors of chocolate and nuts combined with tangy dried cranberries are addictive! They're super sweet, so you may wish to cut them into small squares.

—KARA FIRSTENBERGER CARDIFF, CA

PREP: 15 MIN. • **BAKE:** 30 MIN. + COOLING • **MAKES:** 2 DOZEN

1 **package yellow cake mix (regular size)**
1 **egg**
½ **cup butter, melted**
1 **cup dried cranberries**
1 **cup coarsely chopped cashews**
1 **cup butterscotch chips**

1 **cup semisweet chocolate chips**
1 **can (14 ounces) sweetened condensed milk**

1. In a large bowl, beat cake mix, egg and butter until combined. Press into a greased 13-in. x 9-in. baking pan. Bake at 375° for 10 minutes.

2. Sprinkle the cranberries, cashews and chips over warm crust. Drizzle with milk. Bake 18-20 minutes longer or until golden brown. Cool completely on a wire rack. Cut into bars.

COOKIES & BARS {187}

LEMON-POPPY SEED CUTOUT COOKIES

My recipe for lemon poppy seed biscotti is made from cake mix and I like the flavor. I had seen a recipe for making cookies from cake mix, too, so I reached for my favorite combo again and made a lemon poppy seed version. My cutout recipe makes a crisp cookie, not a cake-like one. If you like, you can omit the refrigeration step and, after mixing, drop the batter by teaspoon onto a cookie sheet and bake for 10 minutes.

—CHARLOTTE MCDANIEL JACKSONVILLE, AL

PREP: 30 MIN. + CHILLING • **BAKE:** 10 MIN./BATCH • **MAKES:** 3 DOZEN

- 1 **package lemon cake mix (regular size)**
- ½ **cup canola oil**
- 2 **eggs**
- ¼ **cup poppy seeds**
- ¾ **teaspoon grated lemon peel**

1. In a large bowl, combine the cake mix, oil and eggs until well blended. Stir in poppy seeds and lemon peel.

2. Divide dough in half. Shape each into a ball, then flatten into a disk. Wrap in plastic wrap and refrigerate for 2 hours or until easy to handle.

3. On a lightly floured surface, roll one portion of dough to ⅛-in. thickness. Cut with a floured 2¼-in. cookie cutter. Place 2 in. apart on greased baking sheets. Repeat.

4. Bake at 375° for 9-11 minutes or until edges are lightly browned. Remove to wire racks to cool completely. Store in an airtight container.

FAST FIX ▸ CHEWY CARAMEL BARS

There are always requests for this favorite recipe wherever it goes! The Rolo candies make them extra gooey and good.

—DEBRA DAVIDSON-CREGEUR HARBOR BEACH, MI

PREP: 10 MIN. • **BAKE:** 40 MIN. + COOLING • **MAKES:** 2 DOZEN

- 1 **package yellow cake mix (regular size)**
- 1 **can (5 ounces) evaporated milk**
- ¼ **cup butter, melted**
- ½ **cup chopped nuts**
- 36 **Rolo candies, halved**

1. Preheat oven to 350°. In a large bowl, beat the cake mix, milk and butter until blended (batter will be thick). Stir in nuts. Press half of mixture into a 13x9-in. baking pan coated with cooking spray. Bake 10-12 minutes or until set.

2. Place candies, cut side down, over crust. Drop remaining batter by tablespoonfuls over the top. Bake 25-30 minutes longer or until golden brown. Cool on a wire rack. Cut into bars.

GERMAN CHOCOLATE THUMBPRINT COOKIES

I love anything with the combination of German chocolate, pecans and coconut.
The taste is most often associated with cake...until now!

—KATHLEEN MORROW HUBBARD, OH

PREP: 45 MIN. + CHILLING • **BAKE:** 10 MIN./BATCH • **MAKES:** 5 DOZEN

- 1 **cup sugar**
- 1 **cup evaporated milk**
- ½ **cup butter, cubed**
- 3 **egg yolks**
- 1½ **cups flaked coconut**
- 1½ **cups chopped pecans**
- 1 **teaspoon vanilla extract**
- 1 **package German chocolate cake mix (regular size)**
- ½ **cup all-purpose flour**
- ⅓ **cup butter, melted**

1. In a large heavy saucepan, combine the sugar, milk, butter and egg yolks. Cook and stir over medium-low heat until mixture is thickened and coats the back of a spoon. Remove from the heat. Stir in the coconut, pecans and vanilla. Set aside 1¼ cups for topping.

2. In a large bowl, combine the cake mix, flour, melted butter and remaining coconut mixture. Cover and refrigerate for at least 1 hour.

3. Shape dough into 1-in. balls. Place 2 in. apart on greased baking sheets. Using the end of a wooden spoon handle, make an indentation in the center of each cookie. Fill each cookie with a teaspoonful of reserved topping.

4. Bake cookies at 350° for 10-12 minutes or until set. Let stand for 2 minutes before removing to wire racks to cool. Store in an airtight container.

FAST FIX ▸ CARAMEL-PECAN DREAM BARS

These ooey-gooey cake bars that pull ever so gently from the pan and hold a firm cut are a baker's dream come true.

—CAY KEPPERS NISSWA, MN

PREP: 15 MIN. • **BAKE:** 20 MIN. + COOLING • **MAKES:** 2 DOZEN

1 **package yellow cake mix (regular size)**
½ **cup butter, softened**
1 **egg**

FILLING

1 **can (14 ounces) sweetened condensed milk**
1 **egg**

1 **teaspoon vanilla extract**
1 **cup chopped pecans**
½ **cup brickle toffee bits**

1. Preheat oven to 350°. In a large bowl, beat the cake mix, butter and egg until crumbly. Press onto the bottom of a greased 13x9-in. baking pan.

2. In a small bowl, beat milk, egg and vanilla until combined. Stir in pecans and toffee bits. Pour over crust.

3. Bake 20-25 minutes or until golden brown. Cool on a wire rack. Cut into bars.

MACADAMIA SUNSHINE BARS

Your guests will be delighted with my bars. They're packed with nuts and dried fruit.
I think that when you take a bite of this treat it's like a minivacation to a Polynesian paradise.
—**JEANNE HOLT** MENDOTA HEIGHTS, MN

PREP: 20 MIN. • **BAKE:** 35 MIN. + COOLING • **MAKES:** 2 DOZEN

- 1 **package lemon cake mix (regular size)**
- ⅔ **cup packed light brown sugar**
- ½ **teaspoon Chinese five-spice powder**
- ¾ **cup butter, melted**
- 2 **eggs**
- 4½ **teaspoons thawed pineapple-orange juice concentrate**
- 2 **teaspoons grated orange peel**
- 2 **teaspoons grated lemon peel**
- ½ **teaspoon vanilla extract**
- 2 **jars (3 ounces each) macadamia nuts, coarsely chopped**

- ⅔ **cup coarsely chopped shelled pistachios**
- ⅔ **cup chopped dried pineapple**
- ⅔ **cup chopped dried mangoes**
- ⅓ **cup flaked coconut, toasted**

GLAZE
- 1¼ **cups confectioners' sugar**
- 1½ **teaspoons thawed pineapple-orange juice concentrate**
- 4 **to 5 teaspoons water**

1. In large bowl, combine the cake mix, brown sugar and spice powder. Add the butter, eggs, juice concentrate, orange and lemon peels and vanilla; beat on medium speed for 2 minutes. Stir in nuts, dried fruits and coconut.
2. Spread batter into a greased 13x9-in. baking pan. Bake at 350° for 35-40 minutes or until a toothpick inserted near the center comes out clean. Cool completely on a wire rack.
3. Combine confectioners' sugar, juice concentrate and enough water to reach a drizzling consistency; drizzle over top. Cut into bars.

FAST FIX LEMON ANGEL CAKE BARS

A neighbor gave me this recipe years ago and it's been in flavor rotation ever since.
It can be made ahead and serves a bunch, so it's perfect for parties and potlucks.
—**MARINA CASTLE** CANYON COUNTRY, CA

PREP: 15 MIN. • **BAKE:** 20 MIN. + CHILLING • **MAKES:** 4 DOZEN

- 1 **package (16 ounces) angel food cake mix**

- 1 **can (15¾ ounces) lemon pie filling**
- 1 **cup finely shredded unsweetened coconut**

FROSTING
- 1 **package (8 ounces) cream cheese, softened**
- ½ **cup butter, softened**
- 1 **teaspoon vanilla extract**
- 2½ **cups confectioners' sugar**
- 3 **teaspoons grated lemon peel**

1. Preheat oven to 350°. In a bowl, mix cake mix, pie filling and coconut until blended; spread into a greased 15x10x1-in. baking pan.

2. Bake 20-25 minutes or until toothpick inserted in center comes out clean. Cool completely in pan on a wire rack.
3. Meanwhile, in a large bowl, beat cream cheese, butter and vanilla until smooth. Gradually add confectioners' sugar. Spread over cooled bars; sprinkle with lemon peel. Refrigerate, covered, at least 4 hours. Cut into bars or triangles.
NOTE *Look for unsweetened coconut in the baking or health food section.*

SWEET POTATO CHEESECAKE BARS

Your whole house will be filled with the aroma of pumpkin spice when you bake these wonderful bars. They look complicated but are so simple you can whip up a batch anytime.

—NANCY WHITFORD EDWARDS, NY

PREP: 20 MIN. • **BAKE:** 25 MIN. + CHILLING • **MAKES:** 2 DOZEN

- 1 **package yellow cake mix (regular size)**
- ½ **cup butter, softened**
- 1 **egg**

FILLING

- 1 **can (15 ounces) sweet potatoes, drained**
- 1 **package (8 ounces) cream cheese, cubed**
- ½ **cup plus ¼ cup sugar, divided**
- 1 **egg**
- 1½ **teaspoons pumpkin pie spice**
- 1 **cup (8 ounces) sour cream**
- ¼ **teaspoon vanilla extract**

TOPPING

- 1¼ **cups granola without raisins**
- ½ **cup white baking chips**
- ¼ **teaspoon pumpkin pie spice**

1. In a large bowl, beat the cake mix, butter and egg until crumbly. Press onto the bottom of a greased 13x9-in. baking dish.

2. Place the sweet potatoes, cream cheese, ½ cup sugar, egg and pie spice in a food processor; cover and process until blended. Spread over crust.

3. Bake at 350° for 20-25 minutes or until center is almost set. Meanwhile, in a small bowl combine the sour cream, vanilla and remaining sugar. Spread over the filling. Combine the topping ingredients; sprinkle over top. Bake 5-8 minutes longer or just until set. Cool on a wire rack.

4. Refrigerate for at least 2 hours. Cut into bars. Store in the refrigerator.

YUMMY COOKIE BARS

I received this recipe from a special co-worker at school, and I always feel like a huge success as the tasty bars turn out every time. I find they're easier to cut if you make them a day in advance and let them sit overnight.

—TERESA HAMMAN SLAYTON, MN

PREP: 20 MIN. • **BAKE:** 25 MIN. + COOLING • **MAKES:** 2 DOZEN

- 1 **package white cake mix (regular size)**
- ½ **cup canola oil**
- 2 **eggs**
- ½ **cup butter, cubed**
- ½ **cup milk chocolate chips**
- ½ **cup peanut butter chips**
- 1 **can (14 ounces) sweetened condensed milk**

1. In a large bowl, combine the cake mix, oil and eggs. Press half of dough into a greased 13x9-in. baking pan.

2. In a small microwave-safe bowl, melt butter and chips; stir until smooth. Stir in milk. Pour over crust. Drop remaining dough by teaspoonfuls over the top.

3. Bake at 350° for 25-30 minutes or until edges are golden brown. Cool completely on a wire rack before cutting into bars.

CAN'T LEAVE ALONE BARS

I bring these swift and simple treats to church meetings, potlucks and housewarming parties. I often make a double batch so we can enjoy some at home.
—**KIMBERLY BIEL** JAVA, SD

PREP: 20 MIN.
BAKE: 20 MIN. + COOLING
MAKES: 3 DOZEN

- **1 package white cake mix (regular size)**
- **2 eggs**
- **⅓ cup canola oil**
- **1 can (14 ounces) sweetened condensed milk**
- **1 cup (6 ounces) semisweet chocolate chips**
- **¼ cup butter, cubed**

1. In a large bowl, combine the cake mix, eggs and oil. Press two-thirds of the mixture into a greased 13x9-in. baking pan. Set remaining cake mixture aside.

2. In a microwave-safe bowl, combine the milk, chocolate chips and butter. Microwave, uncovered, until chips and butter are melted; stir until smooth. Pour over the crust. Drop teaspoonfuls of remaining cake mixture over top.

3. Bake at 350° for 20-25 minutes or until lightly browned. Cool completely on a wire rack. Cut into bars.

NOTE *This recipe was tested in a 1,100-watt microwave.*

PUMPKIN OATMEAL BARS

It took me a long time to perfect this quick recipe, but I'm so pleased with how it turned out.
These bars have it all—sugar and spice and a light, creamy-rich pumpkin layer that's especially nice!

—ERIN ANDREWS EDGEWATER, FL

PREP: 30 MIN. • **BAKE:** 30 MIN. + COOLING • **MAKES:** 2 DOZEN

1 package yellow cake mix (regular size)
2½ cups quick-cooking oats
5 tablespoons butter, melted
3 tablespoons honey
1 tablespoon water

FILLING

1 can (15 ounces) solid-pack pumpkin
¼ cup reduced-fat cream cheese
¼ cup fat-free milk
3 tablespoons brown sugar
2 tablespoons maple syrup
1 teaspoon ground cinnamon
1 teaspoon vanilla extract
¼ teaspoon ground allspice
¼ teaspoon ground cloves
1 egg
1 egg white
¼ cup chopped walnuts
1 tablespoon butter, melted

1. In a large bowl, combine cake mix and oats; set aside ½ cup for topping. Add the butter, honey and water to the remaining cake mixture. Press onto the bottom of a 13x9-in. baking pan coated with cooking spray.

2. For filling, in a large bowl, beat the pumpkin, cream cheese, milk, brown sugar, maple syrup, cinnamon, vanilla, allspice and cloves until blended. Add egg and egg white; beat on low speed just until combined. Pour over crust. In a small bowl, combine the walnuts, butter and reserved cake mixture; sprinkle over filling.

3. Bake at 350° for 30-35 minutes or until set and edges are lightly browned. Cool on a wire rack. Cut into bars.

CHOCOLATE CHIP
PUMPKIN BARS

FAST FIX EASY CHOCOLATE CHIP PUMPKIN BARS

This dessert is super easy to pull together and the flavorful results will win you nothing but compliments.

—AIMEE RANSOM HOSCHTON, GA

PREP: 5 MIN. • **BAKE:** 30 MIN. • **MAKES:** 3 DOZEN

1 **package spice cake mix (regular size)**
1 **can (15 ounces) solid-pack pumpkin**
2 **cups (12 ounces) semisweet chocolate chips, divided**

1. In a large bowl, combine cake mix and pumpkin; beat on low speed for 30 seconds. Beat on medium for 2 minutes. Fold in 1½ cups chocolate chips. Spread in a greased 13x9-in. baking pan.

2. Bake at 350° for 30-35 minutes or until toothpick inserted in center comes out clean. Cool completely in pan on a wire rack.

3. In a microwave, melt the remaining chocolate chips; stir until smooth. Drizzle over bars. Let stand until set.

FAST FIX ANGEL MACAROONS

My chewy coconut cookies start with an angel food cake mix. A fresh-baked batch always disappears in a flash.

—RENEE SCHWEBACH DUMONT, MN

PREP: 5 MIN. • **BAKE:** 10 MIN./BATCH + COOLING • **MAKES:** 5 DOZEN

1 **package (16 ounces) angel food cake mix**
½ **cup water**
1½ **teaspoons almond extract**
2 **cups flaked coconut**

1. In a large bowl, beat the cake mix, water and extract on low speed for 30 seconds. Scrape bowl; beat on medium speed for 1 minute. Fold in the coconut.

2. Drop by rounded teaspoonfuls 2 in. apart onto a parchment paper-lined baking sheet.

3. Bake at 350° for 10-12 minutes or until lightly browned. Remove paper with cookies to wire racks to cool.

BLUEBERRY CRUMB BARS

Think of this as a warm pan of blueberry crisp turned into a hand-held treat.
Oats and fresh blueberries join up to create a sweet, no-fuss dish.

—BLAIR LONERGAN ROCHELLE, VA

PREP: 20 MIN. • **BAKE:** 20 MIN. + COOLING • **MAKES:** 1 DOZEN

- 1 **package yellow cake mix (regular size)**
- 2½ **cups old-fashioned oats**
- ¾ **cup butter, melted**
- 1 **jar (12 ounces) blueberry preserves**
- ⅓ **cup fresh blueberries**
- 1 **tablespoon lemon juice**
- ⅓ **cup finely chopped pecans**
- 1 **teaspoon ground cinnamon**

1. In a large bowl, combine the cake mix, oats and butter until crumbly. Press 3 cups into a greased 9-in. square baking pan. Bake at 350° for 15 minutes. Cool on a wire rack for 5 minutes.

2. Meanwhile, in a small bowl, combine preserves, blueberries and lemon juice. Spread over crust. Stir pecans and cinnamon into remaining crumb mixture. Sprinkle over top.

3. Bake for 18-20 minutes or until lightly browned. Cool completely on a wire rack. Cut into bars.

BUTTERSCOTCH TOFFEE COOKIES

My cookie with its big butterscotch flavor stands out at events among all the chocolate. Of course, I like to enjoy it with a glass of milk or a cup of coffee. It's my fall-back recipe when I'm short on time and need something delicious fast.

—ALLIE BLINDER NORCROSS, GA

PREP: 10 MIN. • **BAKE:** 10 MIN./BATCH
MAKES: 5 DOZEN

- 2 **eggs**
- ½ **cup canola oil**
- 1 **package butter pecan cake mix (regular size)**
- 1 **package (10 to 11 ounces) butterscotch chips**
- 1 **package (8 ounces) milk chocolate English toffee bits**

1. In a large bowl, beat eggs and oil until blended; gradually add cake mix and mix well. Fold in chips and toffee bits.

2. Drop by tablespoonfuls 2 in. apart onto greased baking sheets. Bake at 350° for 10-12 minutes or until golden brown. Cool for 1 minute before removing to wire racks.

FAST FIX ▶ RASPBERRY OATMEAL BARS

Cake mix hurries along the prep work for these yummy bars. Raspberry jam adds a pop of color and sweetness, and oats lend a homey touch.
—TRISH BOSMAN-GOLATA ROCK HILL, SC

PREP: 10 MIN. • **BAKE:** 35 MIN. + COOLING • **MAKES:** 2 DOZEN

- 1 **package yellow cake mix (regular size)**
- 2½ **cups quick-cooking oats**
- ¾ **cup butter, melted**
- 1 **jar (12 ounces) seedless raspberry preserves**
- 1 **tablespoon water**

1. In a large bowl, combine the cake mix, oats and butter until crumbly. Press 3 cups of the crumb mixture into a greased 13x9-in. baking pan. Bake at 350° for 10 minutes. Cool on a wire rack for 5 minutes.

2. In a small bowl, stir preserves and water until blended. Spread over crust. Sprinkle with the remaining crumb mixture.

3. Bake for 25-28 minutes or until lightly browned. Cool on a wire rack. Cut into bars.

GIANT SPICE COOKIES

Around the 1950s this recipe was given out on a radio show I was listening to. It sounded so good, I wrote down the directions. These goodies remain my favorite to this day.
—SANDY PYEATT ROCKAWAY BEACH, OR

PREP: 20 MIN. • **BAKE:** 15 MIN. + COOLING • **MAKES:** 10 COOKIES

- 1 **package spice cake mix (regular size)**
- ½ **teaspoon ground ginger**
- ¼ **teaspoon baking soda**
- ¼ **cup water**
- ¼ **cup molasses**
- 6 **teaspoons vanilla extract**

1. In a large bowl, combine the cake mix, ginger and baking soda. Stir in water, molasses and vanilla and mix well. Roll into 10 balls.

2. Place the ballls 3 in. apart on greased baking sheets. Flatten slightly with a glass coated with cooking spray.

3. Bake at 375° for 13-15 minutes or until the surface cracks and cookies are firm. Remove to wire racks to cool.

FAST FIX MORE THE MERRIER ORANGE, FIG & WALNUT BARS

Orange, figs and walnuts make a bar that's uniquely delicious. Think you can eat just one?

—**JUDY DALTON** DANVILLE, VA

PREP: 10 MIN. • **BAKE:** 25 MIN. • **MAKES:** 3 DOZEN

- 1 **package orange cake mix (regular size)**
- 1 **jar (10 ounces) fig preserves**
- ½ **cup canola oil**
- 1 **egg**
- 2 **cups chopped walnuts**

1. In a large bowl, combine the cake mix, preserves, oil and egg; beat on low speed until blended. Stir in walnuts. (Batter will be thick.) Spread into a greased 13x9-in. baking pan.

2. Bake at 350° for 25-30 minutes or until a toothpick inserted in center comes out clean. Cool on a wire rack. Cut into bars.

{8}

Desserts & More

209

Deluxe Strawberry Shortcake

212

Chocolate Trifle

220

Pumpkin Walnut Squares

COCONUT RHUBARB DESSERT

What a treat! Sweetened rhubarb combines with crunchy pecans and flaked coconut, while a cake mix creates a tender base.

—CONNIE KORGER GREEN BAY, WI

PREP: 25 MIN. • **BAKE:** 25 MIN. • **MAKES:** 12 SERVINGS

- 4 **cups sliced fresh or frozen rhubarb**
- 1½ **cups sugar**
- 1½ **cups water**
- ⅛ **teaspoon red food coloring, optional**
- 1 **package butter pecan cake mix (regular size)**
- 1 **cup flaked coconut**
- ½ **cup chopped pecans**
- ½ **cup butter, melted**
  Vanilla ice cream, optional

1. Preheat oven to 350°. In a large saucepan, combine rhubarb, sugar, water and food coloring if desired. Cook over medium heat for 8-10 minutes or until rhubarb is tender; cool slightly. Transfer to a greased 13x9-in. baking dish; sprinkle with cake mix. Top with the coconut and pecans. Drizzle with butter.

2. Bake 25-30 minutes or until a toothpick inserted in the center comes out clean. Serve with ice cream if desired.

STRAWBERRY ANGEL TRIFLE

I always get compliments when I bring this attractive and tasty trifle out of the refrigerator. Not only does it serve a big group nicely, I can make it ahead of time, too.

—LUCILLE BELSHAM FORT FRASER, BC

PREP: 30 MIN. + CHILLING • **BAKE:** 35 MIN. • **MAKES:** 12-16 SERVINGS

- 1 **package (16 ounces) angel food cake mix**
- 2 **packages (3 ounces each) strawberry gelatin**
- ¾ **cup plus ⅓ cup sugar, divided**
- 2 **cups boiling water**
- 5 **cups fresh or frozen unsweetened strawberries, thawed and drained**
- 2 **cups heavy whipping cream**

1. Prepare and bake cake mix according to package directions; cool completely.

2. In a large bowl, dissolve gelatin and ¾ cup sugar in boiling water. Mash half of the strawberries; add to gelatin mixture. Refrigerate until slightly thickened, about 1 hour. Slice the remaining strawberries; stir into the gelatin.

3. Cut cake into 1-in. cubes. Place half in a 3-qt. trifle or glass bowl. Top with half of the gelatin mixture. Repeat. Cover and refrigerate until set, about 4 hours. In a bowl, beat cream until soft peaks form. Gradually add remaining sugar, beating until stiff peaks form. Spoon over the gelatin.

CINNAMON ROLLS

I serve these yummy frosted rolls warm from the oven as a Christmas morning treat at our house. Even if you are not accustomed to working with yeast dough, you'll find this one is easy to handle.

—JULIE STERCHI JACKSON, MO

PREP: 30 MIN. + RISING • **BAKE:** 10 MIN. + COOLING • **MAKES:** 2 DOZEN

- 5 **to 6 cups all-purpose flour**
- 1 **package yellow cake mix (regular size)**
- 2 **packages (¼ ounce each) quick-rise yeast**
- 2½ **cups warm water (120° to 130°)**
- ¼ **cup butter, melted**
- ½ **cup sugar**
- 1 **teaspoon ground cinnamon**

FROSTING
- 6 **tablespoons butter, softened**
- 3 **cups confectioners' sugar**
- 1½ **teaspoons vanilla extract**
- 2 **to 3 tablespoons 2% milk**

1. In a large bowl, combine 4 cups flour, cake mix, yeast and warm water until smooth. Add enough remaining flour to form a soft dough.

2. Turn onto a lightly floured surface; knead until smooth and elastic, about 5 minutes. Place in a greased bowl, turning once to grease top. Cover and let rise until doubled, about 45 minutes.

3. Punch dough down. Turn onto a lightly floured surface; divide in half. Roll each portion into a 14x10-in. rectangle. Brush with butter; sprinkle with sugar and cinnamon.

4. Roll up jelly-roll style, starting with a long side. Cut each roll into 12 slices; place cut side down in two greased 13x9-in. baking pans. Cover and let rise until almost doubled, about 20 minutes.

5. Bake at 400° for 10-15 minutes or until golden brown. Cool for 20 minutes.

6. For frosting, in a large bowl, cream the butter, confectioners' sugar and vanilla and enough milk to achieve desired consistency. Frost warm rolls.

DELUXE STRAWBERRY SHORTCAKE

This tasty shortcake is perfect for springtime gatherings. I love the moist, from-scratch flavor of the cake.
It's foolproof and always brings lots of compliments.

—JANET FANT DENAIR, CA

PREP: 25 MIN. • **BAKE:** 20 MIN. + COOLING • **MAKES:** 12 SERVINGS

- 1 **package yellow cake mix (regular size)**
- 1 **cup water**
- ½ **cup sour cream**
- ⅓ **cup canola oil**
- 3 **eggs**
- 1 **teaspoon vanilla extract**

FILLING

- 1 **package (8 ounces) cream cheese, softened**
- ⅓ **cup sugar**
- 1 **carton (8 ounces) frozen whipped topping, thawed**
- 3 **cups chopped fresh strawberries**
   Fresh mint leaves, optional

1. In a large bowl, combine the first six ingredients; beat on low speed for 30 seconds. Beat on medium for 2 minutes. Pour into two greased and floured 9-in. round baking pans.

2. Bake at 350° for 20-25 minutes or until a toothpick inserted near the center comes out clean. Cool for 10 minutes before removing from the pans to wire racks to cool completely.

3. In a small bowl, beat cream cheese and sugar until smooth. Fold in whipped topping. Place one cake on a serving plate; top with half of the cream cheese mixture and strawberries. Repeat layers. Store in the refrigerator. Garnish with fresh mint leaves if desired.

PUMPKIN PECAN LOAVES

The bread is too good not to share! Three loaves easily feed a crowd, or you can use them as gifts. Either way, these spice-swirled loaves get gobbled up fast.

—ROBIN GUTHRIE VICTORVILLE, CA

PREP: 20 MIN. • **BAKE:** 45 MIN. + COOLING • **MAKES:** 3 LOAVES (12 SLICES EACH)

- ¾ cup packed brown sugar
- ½ cup all-purpose flour
- ⅓ cup cold butter, cubed
- 1 cup chopped pecans, divided
- 2 packages (16 ounces each) pound cake mix
- 1 can (15 ounces) solid-pack pumpkin
- 4 eggs
- ¾ cup water
- 2 teaspoons baking soda
- 2 teaspoons pumpkin pie spice

1. For streusel, combine brown sugar and flour in a bowl; cut in butter until mixture resembles coarse crumbs. Stir in ½ cup pecans; set aside.

2. In a large bowl, combine the pound cake mixes, pumpkin, eggs, water, baking soda and pumpkin pie spice; beat on low speed for 30 seconds. Beat on medium for 2 minutes. Fold in remaining pecans.

3. Divide half of the batter among three greased and floured 8x4-in. loaf pans. Sprinkle with half of the streusel. Top with the remaining batter and streusel.

4. Bake at 350° for 45-50 minutes or until a toothpick inserted near the center comes out clean. Cool for 10 minutes before removing from the pans to wire racks to cool completely.

FAST FIX▶ BLUEBERRY COBBLER

This simple-to-make dessert comes together in a jiffy. If you like, you can substitute other pie filling, such as apple or cherry for the blueberry.

—NELDA CRONBAUGH BELLE PLAINE, IA

PREP: 10 MIN. • **COOK:** 3 HOURS • **MAKES:** 6 SERVINGS

- 1 can (21 ounces) blueberry pie filling
- 1 package (9 ounces) yellow cake mix
- ¼ cup chopped pecans
- ¼ cup butter, melted
  Vanilla ice cream, optional

1. Place pie filling in a greased 1½-qt. slow cooker. Sprinkle with cake mix and pecans. Drizzle with butter. Cover and cook on high for 3 hours or until topping is golden brown. Serve warm with the ice cream if desired.

FAST FIX ▸ BANANA NUT BREAD

A yellow cake mix streamlines assembly of this moist golden bread. I searched a long while for a banana bread that was easy to make. This one takes no time at all, and makes two loaves.
—**MARIE DAVIS** PENDLETON, SC

PREP: 10 MIN. • **BAKE:** 40 MIN. + COOLING • **MAKES:** 2 LOAVES (12 SLICES EACH)

---

1 **package yellow cake mix (regular size)**
1 **egg**
½ **cup 2% milk**
1 **cup mashed ripe bananas (about 2 medium)**
½ **cup chopped pecans**

1. In a large bowl, combine the cake mix, egg and milk. Add the bananas; beat on medium speed for 2 minutes. Stir in the pecans. Pour into two greased 8-in. x 4-in. loaf pans.

2. Bake at 350° for 40-45 minutes or until a toothpick inserted near the center comes out clean. Cool for 10 minutes before removing from the pans to wire racks to cool completely.

CHOCOLATE TRIFLE

For a fabulous finale when entertaining, this lovely layered trifle is a winner! It's a do-ahead dessert that serves a group, and even tastes great the next day.
—**PAM BOTINE** GOLDSBORO, NC

PREP: 30 MIN. + CHILLING • **MAKES:** 8-10 SERVINGS

---

1 **package chocolate fudge cake mix (regular size)**
1 **package (6 ounces) instant chocolate pudding mix**
½ **cup strong coffee**
1 **carton (12 ounces) frozen whipped topping, thawed**
6 **Heath candy bars (1.4 ounces each), crushed**

1. Bake the cake according to the package directions. Cool. Prepare pudding according to the package directions; set aside.

2. Crumble cake; reserve ½ cup. Place half of the remaining cake crumbs in the bottom of a 4½- or 5-qt. trifle dish or decorative glass bowl.

3. Layer with half of the coffee, half of the pudding, half of the whipped topping and half of the crushed candy bars. Repeat the layers of cake, coffee, pudding and whipped topping.

4. Mix remaining crushed candy bars with reserved cake crumbs; sprinkle over the top. Refrigerate 4-5 hours before serving.

HOLIDAY ENGLISH TRIFLES

Here's a recipe that has everything I want in a holiday dessert. It's yummy, easy to prepare and beautiful.

—BONNIE L. CAMERON COLBERT, WA

PREP: 35 MIN. • **BAKE:** 35 MIN. + CHILLING • **MAKES:** 15 SERVINGS

- 1 **package yellow cake mix (regular size)**
- ⅓ **cup orange juice or orange liqueur**
- ⅓ **cup sherry or additional orange juice**
- 1 **jar (18 ounces) seedless raspberry jam**
- 1½ **cups cold 2% milk**
- 1 **package (3.4 ounces) instant vanilla pudding mix**
- 1 **cup (8 ounces) reduced-fat sour cream**
- 2 **cups heavy whipping cream**
- 3 **tablespoons confectioners' sugar**
- 1½ **cups fresh raspberries**

1. Prepare and bake the cake according to package directions, using a greased 13x9-in. baking pan. Cool; cut into 1-in. cubes.

2. In a small bowl, combine orange juice and sherry. In another bowl, whisk jam. In a large bowl, whisk the milk and pudding mix for 2 minutes. Whisk in the sour cream. Let stand for 2 minutes or until soft-set.

3. Divide half of the cake cubes among 15 parfait glasses or dessert dishes; drizzle with half of the orange juice mixture. Layer each with jam and pudding mixture. Top with remaining cake cubes; drizzle with remaining orange juice mixture. Cover and refrigerate for at least 4 hours or overnight.

4. Just before serving, in a large bowl, beat cream until it begins to thicken. Add the confectioners' sugar; beat until stiff peaks form. Dollop over trifles and garnish with raspberries.

FAST FIX ▸ COUNTRY APPLE DESSERT

If you like warm, comforting sweets, you'll go for my apple dessert. Serve it topped with vanilla ice cream...it's so good!

—DENESE HAROLD DORCAS, WV

PREP: 15 MIN. • **BAKE:** 35 MIN.
MAKES: 15 SERVINGS

- 1 **package yellow cake mix (regular size)**
- ⅓ **cup butter, softened**
- 1 **egg**
- 1 **can (21 ounces) apple pie filling**
- ½ **cup packed brown sugar**
- 1 **teaspoon ground cinnamon**

GLAZE
- ½ **cup confectioners' sugar**
- 1 **tablespoon milk**
- ¼ **teaspoon vanilla extract**
   Vanilla ice cream

1. In a large bowl, beat the cake mix, butter and egg until crumbly. Press onto bottom of a greased 13x9-in. baking pan. Top with the pie filling. Combine the brown sugar and cinnamon; sprinkle over top.

2. Bake at 350° for 35-40 minutes or until golden brown. Cool on a wire rack for 10 minutes. In a small bowl, mix confectioners' sugar, milk and vanilla. Drizzle over the warm cake. Serve with ice cream.

PETER PETER PUMPKIN WHOOPIES

When fall rolls around and it's time for a bake sale, this is the recipe I turn to. The whoopie pies go over wonderfully. The cream cheese filling is perked up with cinnamon and nutmeg. It's perfect with the cakelike outside.

—**DAWN CONTE** SICKLERVILLE, NJ

PREP: 35 MIN. + COOLING • **BAKE:** 10 MIN./BATCH • **MAKES:** 10 WHOOPIE PIES

- 1 **package spice cake mix (regular size)**
- 1¼ **cups canned pumpkin**
- 2 **eggs**
- ½ **cup 2% milk**
- ⅓ **cup butter, softened**

FILLING
- 2 **packages (3 ounces each) cream cheese, softened**
- ½ **cup marshmallow creme**
- ⅓ **cup butter, softened**
- 1½ **cups confectioners' sugar**
- ¾ **teaspoon vanilla extract**
- ½ **teaspoon ground cinnamon**
- ⅛ **teaspoon ground nutmeg**

1. In a large bowl, combine the first five ingredients; beat until well blended. Drop by ¼ cupfuls 3 in. apart onto lightly greased baking sheets.

2. Bake at 375° for 7-10 minutes or until set and edges are lightly browned. Remove to wire racks to cool completely.

3. For filling, in a small bowl, beat the cream cheese, marshmallow creme and butter. Beat in the remaining ingredients. Spread on the bottoms of half of the cookies; top with remaining cookies. Store in the refrigerator.

FAST FIX ► RAISIN POUND CAKE

Yellow cake mix, applesauce and raisins make this moist, spiced loaf a no-fuss favorite. I turn to this cake when unexpected guests drop by because I usually have the ingredients in the pantry. For a special occasion, top slices with fresh fruit.

—**LUELLEN SPAULDING** CARO, MI

PREP: 10 MIN. • **BAKE:** 45 MIN. • **MAKES:** 2 LOAVES (16 SLICES EACH)

- 1 **package yellow cake mix (regular size)**
- 1 **cup applesauce**
- ½ **cup water**
- ¼ **cup canola oil**
- 3 **eggs**
- ½ **teaspoon ground cinnamon**
- ¼ **teaspoon ground nutmeg**
- ¼ **teaspoon ground allspice**
- ½ **cup raisins**

1. In a large bowl, combine cake mix, applesauce, water, oil, eggs, cinnamon, nutmeg and allspice. Beat on medium speed for 2 minutes. Stir in raisins. Pour into two greased 8x4-in. loaf pans.

2. Bake at 350° for 45-50 minutes or until a toothpick inserted near the center comes out clean. Cool for 5-10 minutes before removing from pans to wire racks.

CHOCOLATE-STRAWBERRY BOMBE

Layers of rich devil's food cake and strawberry filling are covered in a heavenly whipped cream frosting.
The treat is sure to satisfy any sweet tooth.

—TASTE OF HOME COOKING SCHOOL

PREP: 20 MIN. + CHILLING • **BAKE:** 20 MIN. • **MAKES:** 16 SERVINGS

- 1 **package devil's food cake mix (regular size)**
- 1 **quart fresh strawberries**
- 2 **envelopes unflavored gelatin**
- ½ **cup thawed strawberry breeze juice concentrate**
- 3 **cups heavy whipping cream, divided**
- 1 **package (8 ounces) cream cheese, softened**
- ½ **cup sugar**
- 1 **tablespoon vanilla extract**
- ½ **cup confectioners' sugar**
- ½ **cup semisweet chocolate chips**
- 1 **teaspoon canola oil**

1. Grease and flour three (8- or 9-in.) round baking pans; set aside. Prepare cake mix batter according to package directions. Divide evenly the batter among prepared pans.

2. Bake at 350° for 22-25 minutes or until a toothpick inserted near center comes out clean. Cool for 10 minutes before removing to wire racks to cool completely.

3. Reserve 6-7 strawberries for garnish. Puree enough of the remaining strawberries to measure 1 cup; set aside. In a small microwave-safe bowl, sprinkle gelatin over juice concentrate; let stand 5 minutes. Microwave on high power 1 minute. Stir until the gelatin is completely dissolved; set aside. In a small]bowl, beat 1 cup

whipping cream until stiff peaks form; set aside.

4. To prepare filling, in a large bowl, beat the cream cheese, sugar and vanilla until smooth. Beat in the strawberry puree. Gradually add gelatin mixture; blend until smooth. Gradually whisk in the whipped cream; set aside.

5. Line a 12-cup bowl with 2-3 long sheets of plastic wrap, allowing ends of plastic to over-hang edges by at least 6 in. (Diameter at top of bowl must be 8½ or 9½ in., depending on size of baking pan.)

6. Gently press one cake layer into bottom of prepared bowl.

7. Spoon about half of filling over cake layer in bowl; top with the second cake layer. Gently press down on cake layer. Spread the

remaining filling over cake. Top with remaining cake layer. Gently press down. Cover cake with loose ends of plastic wrap and refrigerate at least 1 hour.

8. In a small bowl, beat the confectioners' sugar and the remaining cream until stiff peaks form. Uncover top of bombe in bowl. Invert onto serving platter; remove and discard plastic wrap. Frost bombe with sweetened whipped cream.

9. In a microwave, melt chocolate chips with oil; stir until smooth. Transfer to a heavy-duty small reasealable plastic bag. Cut a tiny hole in bottom corner of bag. Gently squeeze bag to drizzle chocolate over the bombe. Garnish as desired with the reserved strawberries.

INDIVIDUAL CRANBERRY TRIFLES

If you don't have enough individual parfaits, you can make this dessert in a trifle bowl. Either way, your crowd will be thrilled!
—**TASTE OF HOME TEST KITCHEN**

PREP: 45 MIN. + CHILLING
MAKES: 14-16 SERVINGS

- 1 package (16 ounces) angel food cake mix
- 2 packages (8 ounces each) cream cheese, softened
- 2 cups confectioners' sugar
- 1 cup (8 ounces) sour cream
- 1 teaspoon vanilla extract
- 1 carton (12 ounces) frozen whipped topping, thawed
- 2 cans (16 ounces each) whole-berry cranberry sauce
- 2 tablespoons sugar
- 2 to 3 teaspoons grated orange peel
  Fresh cranberries or mint, optional

1. Prepare, bake and cool angel food cake according to package directions. Cut into 1-in. cubes; set aside. In a large bowl, mix cream cheese, confectioners' sugar, sour cream and vanilla; beat until smooth. Fold in the whipped topping. In a bowl, combine the cranberry sauce, sugar and orange peel.

2. In individual parfait glasses or a 3-qt. trifle bowl, layer half of the cake cubes, cranberry mixture and whipped topping mixture. Repeat layers. Refrigerate until serving. Garnish with cranberries and mint if desired.

ABC MUFFINS

The ABC abbreviation in these muffin stands for applesauce, bran and cinnamon. My moist bran muffins are an absolute favorite at our house. In fact, my husband asks for them instead of birthday cake.

—**SUSAN SMITH** NEWARK, OH

PREP: 15 MIN. • **BAKE:** 20 MIN. • **MAKES:** 1½ DOZEN

3 eggs
¾ cup canola oil
½ cup applesauce
¼ cup honey
1 package yellow cake mix (regular size)
1½ cups wheat bran
2 teaspoons ground cinnamon

1. In a bowl, beat the eggs, oil, applesauce and honey. Mix cake mix, bran and cinnamon; add to egg mixture. Mix just until blended. Fill greased or paper-lined muffin cups two-thirds full.
2. Bake at 350° for 20-25 minutes or until muffins a toothpick comes out clean. Cool for 5 minutes; remove from pan.

FAST FIX **PUMPKIN WALNUT SQUARES**

My mother-in-law handed this down as a surefire way to keep my husband happy during the holidays. It's his favorite childhood dessert.

—**MELISSA CONCHIERI** JEFFERSON, MA

PREP: 15 MIN. • **BAKE:** 45 MIN. + COOLING • **MAKES:** 12 SERVINGS

1 package yellow cake mix (regular size), divided
¼ cup canola oil
4 eggs
1 cup chopped walnuts, divided
1 can (15 ounces) solid-pack pumpkin
1 can (14 ounces) sweetened condensed milk
1 teaspoon vanilla extract
½ teaspoon salt
½ teaspoon ground cinnamon

1. Set aside ½ cup cake mix for filling. In a bowl, mix oil, 1 egg and remaining cake mix. Press into a greased 13x9-in. baking pan. Sprinkle with ½ cup walnuts.
2. In a large bowl, combine the pumpkin, milk, vanilla, salt, cinnamon, reserved cake mix and remaining eggs. Pour over crust; sprinkle with remaining walnuts.
3. Bake at 350° for 45-50 minutes or until a knife inserted near the center comes out clean. Cool on a wire rack. Cut into squares. Store leftovers in the refrigerator.

OAT APPLE CRISP

A yellow cake mix sets this tasty crisp apart from others. Serve it a la mode for an extra-special treat.

—RUBY HODGE RICHLAND CENTER, WI

PREP: 25 MIN. • **BAKE:** 45 MIN. • **MAKES:** 8 SERVINGS

7 **cups thinly sliced peeled tart apples (about 7 medium)**
1 **cup sugar**
1 **tablespoon all-purpose flour**
1 **teaspoon ground cinnamon**
 Dash salt
¼ **cup water**
1 **package (9 ounces) yellow cake mix**
¾ **cup quick-cooking oats**

⅓ **cup butter, softened**
¼ **cup packed brown sugar**
¼ **teaspoon baking powder**
¼ **teaspoon baking soda**
 Vanilla ice cream

1. Place the apples in a greased 2½- qt. shallow baking dish. In a small bowl, combine the sugar, flour, cinnamon and salt; sprinkle over apples. Drizzle with water. In a large bowl, combine the cake mix, oats, butter, brown sugar, baking powder and baking soda. Sprinkle over apples.

2. Bake, uncovered, at 350° for 45-50 minutes or until the apples are tender and topping is golden brown. Serve warm with the ice cream.

COCONUT-PECAN COFFEE CAKE

I've learned to keep copies of the recipe on hand when I serve this moist and satisfying coffee cake. It has a nice level of coconut flavor from the pudding mix.

—BETH TROPEANO CHARLOTTE, NC

PREP: 15 MIN. • **BAKE:** 35 MIN.
MAKES: 15 SERVINGS

1 **package yellow cake mix (regular size)**
1 **package (3.4 ounces) instant coconut cream pudding mix**
1 **teaspoon vanilla extract**

FILLING

½ **cup chopped pecans**
⅓ **cup sugar**
½ **teaspoon ground cinnamon**

GLAZE

1 **cup confectioners' sugar**
1 **to 2 tablespoons 2% milk**
½ **teaspoon vanilla extract**

1. Prepare the cake mix batter according to package directions, adding pudding mix and vanilla; set aside. In a small bowl, mix the pecans, sugar and cinnamon.

2. Spread half of the cake batter into a greased 13x9-in. baking pan. Sprinkle with half of filling. Top with the remaining batter and filling.

3. Bake at 350° for 34-38 minutes or until a toothpick inserted near the center comes out clean. Cool on a wire rack. In a small bowl, combines the glaze ingredients until smooth. Drizzle over warm coffee cake.

RHUBARB BERRY COFFEE CAKE

For me, the streusel topping adds just the perfect amount of sweetness to the coffee cake, so I omit the frosting.
If you like things a bit sweeter, by all means do top with the frosting.

—JACKIE HEYER CUSHING, IA

PREP: 20 MIN. • **BAKE:** 40 MIN. • **MAKES:** 12-15 SERVINGS

- 1 **package yellow cake mix (regular size), divided**
- ½ **cup packed brown sugar**
- 2 **tablespoons butter**
- ⅔ **cup chopped walnuts**
- 1 **cup (8 ounces) sour cream**
- 2 **eggs**
- ¼ **cup all-purpose flour**
- 1½ **cups finely chopped fresh or frozen rhubarb**
- 1½ **cups sliced fresh strawberries**
- ½ **cup cream cheese frosting, optional**

1. In a small bowl, combine ½ cup cake mix and sugar; cut in butter until crumbly. Add walnuts; set aside.

2. In another bowl, combine the sour cream, eggs, flour and remaining cake mix; beat on low speed for 30 seconds. Beat on medium for 2 minutes. Fold in rhubarb and strawberries. Spread into a greased 13x9-in. baking dish. Sprinkle with reserved crumb mixture.

3. Bake at 350° for 35-40 minutes or until a toothpick inserted near the center comes out clean. Cool on a wire rack.

4. If desired, place frosting in a microwave-safe bowl; heat for 15 seconds. Drizzle over cake.

NOTE *If using frozen rhubarb, measure rhubarb while still frozen, then thaw completely. Drain in a colander, but do not press liquid out.*

{9}

Brownie Treats

228

Brownie Chunk Ice Cream

238

Mint Sundae Brownie Squares

242

Banana Cream Brownie Dessert

ANGELA'S XOXO SHORTBREAD BROWNIES

Everyone loves brownies. This one has a buttery crust with a sweet finish, thanks to the touch of candy on top.

—ANGELA KAMAKANA BAPTISTA HILO, HI

PREP: 20 MIN. + COOLING
BAKE: 25 MIN. • **MAKES:** 16 SERVINGS

- 2 **cups all-purpose flour**
- ½ **cup sugar**
- 1 **cup cold butter, cubed**
- 1 **package fudge brownie mix (13-in. x 9-in. pan size)**
- 8 **striped chocolate kisses, unwrapped**
- 8 **milk chocolate kisses, unwrapped**
- ½ **cup M&M's Minis**

1. In a large bowl, mix flour and sugar; cut in the butter until crumbly. Press onto the bottom of a greased 13x9-in. baking pan. Bake at 350° for 17-20 minutes or until lightly browned. Cool on a wire rack.

2. Prepare the brownie mix batter according to the package directions; spread over the crust. Bake 23-28 minutes longer or until a toothpick inserted in center comes out clean (do not overbake). Immediately top with kisses and M&M's, spacing evenly and pressing down lightly to adhere. Cool in pan on a wire rack.

BROWNIE ALPINE BISCOTTI

Brownie mix makes these crunchy biscotti cookies easy to stir up, and a white chocolate and almond topping adds a special look.

—JEANIE WILLIAMS MINNETONKA, MN

PREP: 25 MIN. • **BAKE:** 40 MIN. + COOLING • **MAKES:** 2½ DOZEN

- 1 **package fudge brownie mix (13-in. x 9-in. size)**
- ¾ **cup ground almonds**
- ½ **cup all-purpose flour**
- ¾ **teaspoon baking powder**
- 1 **egg plus 3 egg whites**
- 1 **teaspoon almond extract**
- ¼ **cup sliced almonds, optional**
- 3 **ounces white baking chocolate, optional**

1. In a large bowl, combine the brownie mix, ground almonds, flour and baking powder. In a small bowl, whisk egg, egg whites and extract. Add to brownie mixture; stir until combined.

2. Divide the dough into thirds. On a greased baking sheet, shape each portion of dough into a 7x3½-in. rectangle. Bake at 350° for 24 minutes. Remove from the oven; cool on baking sheet for 5 minutes.

3. Transfer to a cutting board; cut diagonally with a serrated knife into ¾-in. slices. Place cut side down on greased baking sheets. Bake 12-14 minutes longer or until firm.

4. Cool on wire racks. If desired, sprinkle with sliced almonds and drizzle with chocolate. Let stand until chocolate is completely set. Store in an airtight container.

BROWNIE CHUNK ICE CREAM

Each time I make brownies, half the batch goes to friends and the rest ends up in this ice cream. For crunch, I sometimes add a half-cup of chopped nuts.
—**AGNES WARD** STRATFORD, ON

PREP: 15 MIN.
PROCESSING: 20 MIN./BATCH + FREEZING
MAKES: ABOUT 1½ QUART

- 3 **cups half-and-half cream**
- ¾ **cup sugar, divided**
- 3 **tablespoons baking cocoa**
- 6 **egg yolks**
- 6 **ounces semisweet chocolate, finely chopped**
- 1 **package fudge brownie mix (8-in. square pan size)**

1. In a large saucepan, heat the cream to 175°; stir in ½ cup sugar until dissolved. In a bowl, mix the cocoa and remaining sugar; whisk in egg yolks until smooth. Whisk in a small amount of hot cream mixture. Return all to the pan, whisking constantly. Cook and stir over low heat until mixture reaches at least 160° and coats the back of a metal spoon.
2. Remove from the heat; stir in the chocolate until melted. Cool quickly by placing pan in a bowl of ice water; let stand for 30 minutes, stirring frequently.
3. Transfer to a bowl; press plastic wrap onto surface of custard. Refrigerate for several hours or overnight.

4. Prepare and bake brownies according to package directions. Cool on a wire rack; cut into ½-in. cubes.
5. Fill cylinder of ice cream freezer two-thirds full with custard; freeze according to the manufacturer's directions. Stir in half of the brownie cubes. Refrigerate remaining custard until ready to freeze. Add the remaining brownies. When ice cream is frozen, transfer to a freezer container; freeze for 2-4 hours before serving.

PEANUT BUTTER BROWNIE TRIFLE

This rich, tempting dessert feeds a crowd and features the ever-popular combination of chocolate and peanut butter.

—NANCY FOUST STONEBORO, PA

PREP: 1 HOUR + CHILLING • **MAKES:** 20 SERVINGS (1 CUP EACH)

- 1 **package fudge brownie mix (13-in. x 9-in. pan size)**
- 1 **package (10 ounces) peanut butter chips**
- 2 **packages (13 ounces each) miniature peanut butter cups**
- 4 **cups cold 2% milk**
- 2 **packages (5.1 ounces each) instant vanilla pudding mix**
- 1 **cup creamy peanut butter**
- 4 **teaspoons vanilla extract**
- 3 **cartons (8 ounces each) frozen whipped topping, thawed**

1. Preheat oven to 350°. Prepare brownie batter according to the package directions; stir in peanut butter chips. Bake in a greased 13x9-in. baking pan 20-25 minutes or until a toothpick inserted near the center comes out with moist crumbs. Cool on a wire rack; cut into ¾-in. pieces.

2. Cut the peanut butter cups in half; set aside ⅓ cup for garnish. In a large bowl, whisk milk and pudding mixes for 2 minutes (mixture will be thick). Add the peanut butter and vanilla; mix well. Fold in 1½ cartons whipped topping.

3. Place a third of brownies in a 5-qt. glass bowl; top with a third of remaining peanut butter cups. Spoon a third of pudding mixture over the top. Repeat layers twice. Cover with remaining whipped topping; garnish with reserved peanut butter cups. Refrigerate until chilled.

MAPLE-MOCHA BROWNIE TORTE

Instead of making regular brownies, I bake brownie mix in cake pans to make a quick torte.
Topped with a fluffy maple frosting, this dessert is at the top of my list of speedy standbys.

—AMY FLORY CLEVELAND, GA

PREP: 30 MIN. • **BAKE:** 20 MIN. + COOLING • **MAKES:** 12 SERVINGS

- 1 **package brownie mix (13-in. x 9-in. pan size)**
- ½ **cup chopped walnuts**
- 2 **cups heavy whipping cream**
- 2 **teaspoons instant coffee granules**
- ½ **cup packed brown sugar**
- 1½ **teaspoons maple flavoring**
- 1 **teaspoon vanilla extract**
  Chocolate curls or additional walnuts, optional

1. Preheat oven to 350°. Prepare batter for brownie mix according to package directions for cakelike brownies. Stir in walnuts. Pour into two greased 9-in. round baking pans.

2. Bake 20-22 minutes or until a toothpick inserted 2 in. from edge comes out clean. Cool 10 minutes before removing from pans to wire racks to cool completely.

3. In a large bowl, beat cream and coffee granules until stiff peaks form. Gradually beat in brown sugar, maple flavoring and vanilla.

4. Spread 1½ cups over one brownie layer; top with second layer. Spread remaining cream mixture over top and sides of torte. Garnish with chocolate curls or walnuts if desired. Store in the refrigerator.

FROZEN CHOCOLATE MINT DESSERT

This is adapted from my great-aunt's recipe for grasshopper pie. My last version was a flop, as I put in too much mint extract. I needed to cut the mint taste with something gooey and chocolaty, so I ended up flipping the whole thing upside-down on top of a brownie crust!

—SARAH NEWMAN MAHTOMEDI, MN

PREP: 30 MIN. + FREEZING • **MAKES:** 24 SERVINGS

- **1 package fudge brownie mix (13-in. x 9-in. pan size)**
- **2 egg whites**
- **¼ cup unsweetened applesauce**
- **2 teaspoons vanilla extract**
- **½ cup baking cocoa**
- **1½ cups fat-free milk**
- **2 package (16 ounces each) large marshmallows**
- **½ teaspoon mint extract**
- **1 carton (16 ounces) frozen reduced-fat whipped topping, thawed**

- **⅔ cup cream-filled chocolate sandwich cookie crumbs**

1. In a large bowl, mix brownie mix, egg whites, applesauce and vanilla. Spread into a 13x9-in. baking dish coated with cooking spray. Bake at 350° for 18-22 minutes or until a toothpick inserted near the center comes out clean. Cool on a wire rack.

2. In a Dutch oven, combine the cocoa and milk. Cook and stir over medium heat until the cocoa is dissolved. Stir in marshmallows until melted. Remove from heat; stir in extract. Cool completely.

3. Fold in the whipped topping. Spread over brownies. Sprinkle with the cookie crumbs. Cover and freeze for at least 8 hours. Remove from freezer 10 minutes before serving.

DIPPED BROWNIE POPS

I needed to have a quick fundraiser for the student organization at my school,
so I made these pops. The kids loved them and I sold over 200 hundred in an afternoon !

—JAMIE FRANKLIN MURTAUGH, ID

PREP: 45 MIN. • **BAKE:** 35 MIN. + COOLING • **MAKES:** 16 BROWNIE POPS

- 1 **package fudge brownie mix (13-in. x 9-in. pan size)**
- 16 **Popsicle sticks**
- ⅔ **cup semisweet chocolate chips**
- 3 **teaspoons shortening, divided**
- ⅔ **cup white baking chips**
  Assorted sprinkles, chopped pecans and/or miniature marshmallows

1. Line a 8- or 9-in. square baking pan with foil; grease the foil and set aside. Prepare and bake brownie mix according to the package directions for the size baking pan you used. Cool completely on a wire rack.

2. Using foil, lift brownie out of pan; remove foil. Cut brownie into sixteen squares. Gently insert a Popsicle stick into the side of each square. Cover and freeze for 30 minutes.

3. In a microwave, melt chocolate chips and 1½ teaspoons shortening; stir until smooth. Repeat with the white baking chips and remaining shortening.

4. Dip eight brownies halfway into chocolate mixture; allow excess to drip off. Dip remaining brownies halfway into white chip mixture; allow excess to drip off. Sprinkle with toppings of your choice. Place on waxed paper; let stand until set. Place in bags and fasten with twist ties or ribbon if desired.

TRIPLE-LAYER PRETZEL BROWNIES

Think of a brownie pie with a pretzel crust and peanut butter-chocolate
topping. Now stop thinking about it and make it happen.

—CATHIE AYERS HILTON, NY

PREP: 30 MIN. • **BAKE:** 35 MIN. + COOLING • **MAKES:** 2 DOZEN

- 3 **cups crushed pretzels**
- ¾ **cup butter, melted**
- 3 **tablespoons sugar**
- 1 **package fudge brownie mix (13-in. x 9-in. pan size)**
- ¾ **cup semisweet chocolate chips**
- ½ **cup creamy peanut butter**

1. Preheat oven to 400°. In a small bowl, combine pretzels, butter and sugar. Press into an ungreased 13x9-in. baking dish. Bake 8 minutes. Cool on a wire rack.

2. Reduce heat to 350°. Prepare brownie mix batter according to package directions. Pour over prepared crust. Bake 35-40 minutes or until a toothpick inserted near the center comes out with moist crumbs (do not overbake). Cool completely on a wire rack.

3. In a microwave, melt the chocolate chips and peanut butter; stir until smooth. Spread over top. Refrigerate 30 minutes or until firm. Cut into bars. Store in an airtight container.

RASPBERRY BROWNIE DESSERT

This is such an easy dessert that everyone goes crazy over it! I have brought the treats to church and office potlucks, and everyone always begs for more. The recipe is so easy and goes together in a snap.

—ANN VICK ROSEMOUNT, MN

PREP: 20 MIN.
BAKE: 25 MIN. + CHILLING
MAKES: 15-18 SERVINGS

- 1 package fudge brownie mix (13-in. x 9-in. pan size)
- 2 cups heavy whipping cream, divided
- 1 package (3.3 ounces) instant white chocolate pudding mix
- 1 can (21 ounces) raspberry pie filling

1. Prepare and bake brownies according to the package directions, using a greased 13x9-in. baking pan. Cool completely on a wire rack.
2. In a small bowl, combine 1 cup cream and pudding mix; stir for 2 minutes or until very thick. In a small bowl, beat remaining cream until stiff peaks form; fold into pudding. Carefully spread over brownies; top with the pie filling. Cover and refrigerate for at least 2 hours before cutting.

DOUBLE CHOCOLATE COCONUT BROWNIES

Thanks to a head start from a mix, it's easy to bake up these crowd-pleasing brownies.
It's hard to stop at one, but don't worry, my recipe makes 30 servings!

—**BRENDA MELANCON** MCCOMB, MS

PREP: 15 MIN. • **BAKE:** 40 MIN. + COOLING • **MAKES:** 2½ DOZEN

1 **package fudge brownie mix (13-in. x 9-in. pan size)**
½ **cup canola oil**
¼ **cup water**
3 **eggs**
½ **cup semisweet chocolate chips**
½ **cup white baking chips**
½ **cup chopped walnuts**
1 **can (14 ounces) sweetened condensed milk**
2½ **cups flaked coconut**

FROSTING
¼ **cup butter, softened**
¼ **cup evaporated milk**
2 **tablespoons baking cocoa**
2 **cups confectioners' sugar**
1 **teaspoon vanilla extract**

1. Beat brownie mix, oil, water and eggs on medium speed in a large bowl until blended; stir in chips and walnuts. Pour into a greased 13x9-in. baking pan.

2. Bake at 350° for 20 minutes. Remove from oven. Combine condensed milk and coconut in a small bowl; spread over top. Bake 20-25 minutes longer or until center is set. Cool on a wire rack.

3. Place frosting ingredients in a small bowl; beat until smooth. Spread over cooled brownies.

DECADENT BROWNIE SWIRL CHEESECAKE

It may look fancy, but this cheesecake is so simple to do. The secret is the speedy crust—it's from a packaged mix! You don't need to be an experienced cook to make the elegant chocolate swirls on top.
—**TASTE OF HOME TEST KITCHEN**

PREP: 50 MIN. + COOLING • **BAKE:** 1½ HOURS + CHILLING • **MAKES:** 16 SERVINGS

1 **package fudge brownie mix
(13-in. x 9-in. pan size)**
FILLING
4 **packages (8 ounces each)
cream cheese, softened**
1 **cup sugar**
4 **eggs, lightly beaten**
3 **teaspoons vanilla extract or
1 teaspoon almond extract
and 2 teaspoons vanilla
extract**
**Fresh raspberries and
chocolate curls, optional**

1. Prepare the brownie mix according to package directions for chewy fudge brownies. Set aside ⅔ cup brownie batter; spread remaining batter into a greased 9-in. springform pan.
2. Place pan on a double thickness of heavy-duty foil (about 18 in. square). Securely wrap foil around pan. Bake at 350° for 25-28 minutes (brownies will barely test done). Cool for 10 minutes on a wire rack.
3. In a large bowl, beat cream cheese and sugar until smooth. Beat in eggs and vanilla on low speed just until combined. Stir ⅓ cup into reserved brownie batter; set aside. Spoon half of the cheesecake batter into crust; dollop with half of reserved chocolate cheesecake batter. Repeat layers. Cut through batter with a knife to swirl.

4. Place in a larger baking pan; add 1 in. of hot water to larger pan. Bake at 325° for 1½ hours or until surface is no longer shiny and center is almost set.
5. Remove pan from water bath and foil. Cool on a wire rack for 10 minutes. Carefully run a knife around the edge of pan to loosen; cool 1 hour longer. Refrigerate overnight. Remove sides of pan. Garnish with raspberries and chocolate curls if desired.

BROWNIE CRACKLES

Here's a cookie that uses just sa handful of ingredients, and can be in the oven within 15 minutes. It's the type of go-to recipe busy moms want. Rolling the dough in powdered sugar gives them their inviting crackled appearance.

—ELLEN GOVERTSEN WHEATON, IL

PREP: 15 MIN.
BAKE: 10 MIN./BATCH
MAKES: 4½ DOZEN

- 1 **package fudge brownie mix (13-in. x 9-in. pan size)**
- 1 **cup all-purpose flour**
- 1 **egg**
- ½ **cup water**
- ¼ **cup canola oil**
- 1 **cup (6 ounces) semisweet chocolate chips**
  Confectioners' sugar

1. In a large bowl, beat brownie mix, flour, egg, water and oil until well blended. Stir in the chocolate chips.

2. Place confectioners' sugar in a shallow dish. Drop the dough by tablespoonfuls into sugar; roll to coat.

3. Place 2 in. apart on greased baking sheets. Bake at 350° for 8-10 minutes or until set. Remove from pans to wire racks to cool.

MINT SUNDAE BROWNIE SQUARES

I love brownies, and this recipe makes them into an after-dinner dessert that's just heavenly.

—EDIE DESPAIN LOGAN, UT

PREP: 20 MIN. + FREEZING • **BAKE:** 25 MIN. + COOLING • **MAKES:** 15 SERVINGS

- **1 package fudge brownie mix (13-in. x 9-in. pan size)**
- **¾ cup chopped walnuts**
- **1 can (14 ounces) sweetened condensed milk**
- **2 teaspoons peppermint extract**
- **4 drops green food coloring, optional**
- **2 cups heavy whipping cream, whipped**
- **½ cup miniature semisweet chocolate chips**

- **1 jar (16 ounces) hot fudge ice cream topping, warmed**
- **⅓ cup chopped salted peanuts**

1. Prepare the brownie mix according to package directions. Stir in the walnuts. Pour into a greased 13x9-in. baking pan. Bake at 325° for 23-27 minutes or until a toothpick inserted in the center comes out clean. Cool on a wire rack.

2. Meanwhile, in a large bowl, combine the milk, extract and food coloring if desired. Fold in whipped cream and chocolate chips. Spread over brownie layer. Cover and freeze for several hours or overnight.

3. Let stand at room temperature for 10 minutes before cutting. Drizzle with ice cream topping; sprinkle with peanuts.

PEANUT BUTTER BROWNIE BARS

Here's a no-fuss sweet that will appeal to adults and children alike.
Creamy peanut butter, crunchy nuts and crisp cereal make the bars fun to bite into.

—RADELLE KNAPPENBERGER OVIEDO, FL

PREP: 20 MIN. • **BAKE:** 25 MIN. + CHILLING • **MAKES:** 3 DOZEN

- 1 **package fudge brownie mix (13-in. x 9-in. pan size)**
- 12 **peanut butter cups, chopped**
- ½ **cup salted peanuts, chopped**
- 2 **cups (12 ounces) semisweet chocolate chips**
- 1¼ **cups creamy peanut butter**
- 1 **tablespoon butter**
- 1½ **cups crisp rice cereal**
- 1 **teaspoon vanilla extract**
- ⅛ **teaspoon salt**

1. Prepare the brownie batter according to package directions. Spread into a greased 13x9-in. baking pan. Bake at 350° for 20-25 minutes or until a toothpick inserted near center comes out with moist crumbs.

2. Sprinkle with peanut butter cups and peanuts. Bake 4-6 minutes longer or until chocolate is melted. Cool on a wire rack.

3. Meanwhile, in a microwave, melt the chocolate chips, peanut butter and butter; stir until smooth. Stir in the cereal, vanilla and salt. Carefully spread over brownies. Cover and refrigerate for at least 2 hours before cutting.

CARAMEL FUDGE CHEESECAKE

I combined several recipes to create this dessert that satisfies both the chocolate lovers and the cheesecake lovers in my family. With a fudgy crust, crunchy pecans and a gooey layer of caramel, it's hard to resist.

—BRENDA RUSE TRURO, NS

PREP: 30 MIN. + COOLING • **BAKE:** 35 MIN. + CHILLING • **MAKES:** 12 SERVINGS

- 1 **package fudge brownie mix (8-in. square pan size)**
- 1 **package (14 ounces) caramels**
- ¼ **cup evaporated milk**
- 1¼ **cups coarsely chopped pecans**
- 2 **packages (8 ounces each) cream cheese, softened**
- ½ **cup sugar**
- 2 **eggs, lightly beaten**
- 2 **ounces unsweetened chocolate, melted and cooled**

1. Prepare the brownie batter according to package directions. Spread batter into a greased 9-in. springform pan. Place on a baking sheet. Bake at 350° for 20 minutes. Place pan on a wire rack for 10 minutes (leave oven on).

2. Meanwhile, in a microwave-safe bowl, melt the caramels with milk. Pour over brownie crust; sprinkle with the pecans. In a large bowl, beat the cream cheese and sugar. Add the eggs; beat on low speed just until combined. Stir in the melted chocolate. Pour over pecans. Return pan to baking sheet.

3. Bake for 35-40 minutes or until the center is almost set. Cool on a wire rack for 10 minutes. Run a knife around the edge of pan to loosen; cool 1 hour. Refrigerate overnight. Remove sides of pan. Refrigerate leftovers.

CHOCOLATE-ALMOND BROWNIE PIZZA

Dessert pizza has never been so elegant! Featuring a chewy coconut topping and brownie crust, this treat gives traditional holiday pies and cakes some serious competition.

—PAT CASSITY BOISE, ID

PREP: 10 MIN. • **BAKE:** 35 MIN. + COOLING • **MAKES:** 16 SLICES

1 **package (14 ounces) flaked coconut**
1 **can (14 ounces) sweetened condensed milk**
2 **egg whites**
1 **package fudge brownie mix (13-in. x 9-in. pan size)**
½ **cup sliced almonds**
1 **ounce semisweet chocolate, chopped**
1 **teaspoon canola oil**

1. In a large bowl, combine the coconut, milk and egg whites until blended. Set aside.

2. Prepare the brownie mix according to package directions for fudgelike brownies. Spread onto a greased 12-in. pizza pan.

3. Bake at 375° for 15-18 minutes or until a toothpick inserted near the center comes out clean. Spread coconut mixture over crust to within ½ in. of edges. Sprinkle with almonds. Bake 20-25 minutes longer or until topping is golden brown. Cool completely on a wire rack.

4. In a microwave, melt the chocolate and oil; stir until smooth. Drizzle over pizza.

FAST FIX ▸ MINI BROWNIE TREATS

I like to share these quick-and-easy treats and bring them to any event that requires a dish to pass. They disappear in minutes!

—**PAM KOKES** NORTH LOUP, NE

PREP: 15 MIN. • **BAKE:** 20 MIN. + COOLING • **MAKES:** 4 DOZEN

1 **package fudge brownie mix (13-in. x 9-in. pan size)**
48 **striped or milk chocolate kisses**

1. Prepare the brownie mix according to package directions for fudgelike brownies. Fill paper-lined miniature muffin cups two-thirds full.

2. Bake at 350° for 18-21 minutes or until a toothpick inserted near the center comes out clean.

3. Immediately top each cupcake with a chocolate kiss. Cool for 10 minutes before removing from pans to wire racks to cool completely.

BANANA CREAM BROWNIE DESSERT

I always keep the ingredients for this extremely delicious dessert on hand because I make it quite often for potlucks and family gatherings. I'm always asked for the recipe. After one bite, you'll understand why.

—**JULIE NOWAKOWSKI** LASALLE, IL

PREP: 20 MIN. • **BAKE:** 30 MIN. + COOLING • **MAKES:** 12-15 SERVINGS

1 **package fudge brownie mix (13-in. x 9-in. pan size)**
1 **cup (6 ounces) semisweet chocolate chips, divided**
¾ **cup dry roasted peanuts, chopped, divided**
3 **medium firm bananas**
1⅔ **cups cold milk**
2 **packages (5.1 ounces each) instant vanilla pudding mix**
1 **carton (8 ounces) frozen whipped topping, thawed**

1. Prepare the brownie batter according to package directions for fudgelike brownies. Stir in ½ cup chocolate chips and ¼ cup peanuts. Spread into a greased 13x9-in. baking pan. Bake at 350° for 28-30 minutes or until a toothpick inserted near the center comes out clean. Cool on a wire rack.

2. Slice bananas; arrange in a single layer over brownies.

Sprinkle with ¼ cup chips and ¼ cup peanuts.

3. In a large bowl, beat milk and pudding mixes on low speed for 2 minutes. Fold in whipped topping. Spread over top. Sprinkle with remaining chips and peanuts. Refrigerate until serving.

FUDGY BROWNIES

Rich brownies topped with a peanut butter pudding frosting make a recipe the whole family will love. These are perfect for a bake sale or yummy after-dinner treat.
—**AMY CROOK** SYRACUSE, UT

PREP: 20 MIN.
BAKE: 25 MIN. + CHILLING
MAKES: 2½ DOZEN

- 1 **package fudge brownie mix (13-in. x 9-in. pan size)**
- 1½ **cups confectioners' sugar**
- ½ **cup butter, softened**
- 2 **to 3 tablespoons peanut butter**
- 2 **tablespoons cold 2% milk**
- 4½ **teaspoons instant vanilla pudding mix**
- 1 **can (16 ounces) chocolate fudge frosting**

1. Prepare and bake brownies according to package directions. Cool on a wire rack.

2. Meanwhile, in a small bowl, beat the confectioners' sugar, butter, peanut butter, milk and pudding mix until smooth. Spread over brownies.

3. Refrigerate for 30 minutes or until firm. Frost with chocolate fudge frosting just before cutting.

COBBLESTONE BROWNIES

My family enjoys the combination of chocolate and coconut. So I stirred coconut extract into brownie batter and added flaked coconut to the cream cheese filling. These fudgy bars are the tasty result!

—PHYLLIS PERRY VASSAR, KS

PREP: 15 MIN. • **BAKE:** 55 MIN. + COOLING • **MAKES:** 3 DOZEN

- 1 **package fudge brownie mix (13-in. x 9-in. pan size)**
- ½ **cup canola oil**
- 2 **eggs**
- ½ **teaspoon coconut extract**

FILLING

- 1 **package (8 ounces) cream cheese, softened**
- 2 **eggs**
- 1 **teaspoon coconut extract**
- 1 **teaspoon vanilla extract**
- 3¾ **cups confectioners' sugar**
- 1 **cup flaked coconut**

1. In a large bowl, beat brownie mix, oil, eggs and extract on medium speed until blended (batter will be stiff). Set aside 1 cup for topping.

2. Spread the remaining batter into a greased 13x9-in. baking pan. Bake at 350° for 10-15 minutes or until edges crack.

3. For filling, in a large bowl, beat cream cheese, eggs and extracts until smooth. Gradually add confectioner's sugar and mix well.

Fold in coconut. Carefully spread over brownies.

4. Drop reserved batter by teaspoonfuls over filling. Bake for 45-50 minutes or until a toothpick inserted near the center comes out clean(do not overbake). Cool on a wire rack. Store in the refrigerator.

▶ **PEANUT BUTTER BROWNIE CUPCAKES**

I have made this outstandingly scrumptious recipe for years. These rich treats are so decadent.
—**CAROL GILLESPIE** CHAMBERSBURG, PA

PREP: 15 MIN. • **BAKE:** 15 MIN. + COOLING • **MAKES:** 1 DOZEN

1 **package fudge brownie mix (8-in. square pan size)**
½ **cup miniature semisweet chocolate chips**
⅓ **cup creamy peanut butter**
3 **tablespoon cream cheese, softened**
1 **egg**
¼ **cup sugar**
 Confectioners' sugar

1. Preheat oven to 350°. Prepare brownie batter according to the package directions; stir in the chocolate chips. For filling, in a small bowl, beat the peanut butter, cream cheese, egg and sugar until smooth.

2. Fill paper-lined muffin cups one-third full with batter. Drop filling by teaspoonfuls into the center of each cupcake. Cover with remaining batter.

3. Bake 15-20 minutes or until a toothpick inserted in the brownie portion comes out clean. Cool for 10 minutes before removing from the pan to a wire rack to cool completely. Dust tops with the confectioners' sugar. Store in the refrigerator.

TOFFEE BROWNIE TRIFLE

This delightful combination of pantry items is a terrific way to dress up a brownie mix. Try it with other flavors of pudding, or substitute your favorite candy bar. It tastes great with low-fat and sugar-free products, too.

—WENDY BENNETT SIOUX FALLS, SD

PREP: 20 MIN.
BAKE: 25 MIN. + COOLING
MAKES: 16 SERVINGS

- 1 **package fudge brownie mix (13-in. x 9-in. pan size)**
- 2½ **cups cold milk**
- 1 **package (3.4 ounces) instant cheesecake or vanilla pudding mix**
- 1 **package (3.3 ounces) instant white chocolate pudding mix**
- 1 **carton (8 ounces) frozen whipped topping, thawed**
- 2 **to 3 Heath candy bars (1.4 ounces each), chopped**

1. Prepare and bake brownies according to package directions for cakelike brownies, using a greased 13x9-in. baking pan. Cool completely on a wire rack.

2. In a large bowl, beat milk and pudding mixes on low speed for 2 minutes. Let stand for 2 minutes or until soft-set. Fold in the whipped topping.

3. Cut the brownies into 1-in. cubes. Layer parfait glasses with brownie cubes and pudding. Repeat layers. Sprinkle with chopped candy bars. Refrigerate leftovers.

{ General Index }

{ Alphabetical Index }

Poppy Seed Citrus Cake

Can't Leave Alone Bars

Country Apple Dessert